For CGR.

NEW SCHOOL LEADER
WHAT NOW?

Simple lessons to navigate doubt, embrace challenge and lead well every day

NEIL RENTON

Routledge
Taylor & Francis Group

LONDON AND NEW YORK

First published in 2023 by Critical Publishing Ltd

Published 2025 by Routledge
4 Park Square, Milton Park, Abingdon, Oxon OX14 4RN
605 Third Avenue, New York, NY 10017

*Routledge is an imprint of the Taylor & Francis Group,
an informa business*

Copyright © 2023 Neil Renton

All rights reserved. No part of this publication may be reproduced, stored in a retrieval system, or transmitted in any form or by any means, electronic, mechanical, photocopying, recording or otherwise, without prior permission in writing from the publisher.

Trademark notice: Product or corporate names may be trademarks or registered trademarks, and are used only for identification and explanation without intent to infringe.

British Library Cataloguing in Publication Data
A CIP record for this book is available from the British Library

ISBN: 9781041056294 (hbk)
ISBN: 9781915713421 (pbk)
ISBN: 9781041056287 (ebk)

The right of Neil Renton to be identified as the Author of this work has been asserted by him in accordance with the Copyright, Design and Patents Act 1988.

Text design by Greensplash
Cover design by Out of House Limited

DOI: 10.4324/9781041056287

CONTENTS

Meet the author		viii
Acknowledgements		ix
Endorsements		xi
Introduction		1

PART 1 NAVIGATING DOUBT — 3

Chapter 1	Learning to carry the weight	5
Chapter 2	The importance of allies	7
Chapter 3	Working without praise	10
Chapter 4	Plain speaking	12
Chapter 5	Speaking from the heart	15
Chapter 6	Decisions	18
Chapter 7	U-turns	22
Chapter 8	*Kopfkino*	25
Chapter 9	Forgetting and remembering	28
Chapter 10	Visibility	31
Chapter 11	Asking for help	33
Part 1 summary		36

PART 2 EMBRACING CHALLENGE — 41

Chapter 12	Facing significant underperformance head-on	43
Chapter 13	Covering off in a crisis	45
Chapter 14	Assertion	48
Chapter 15	Keeping perspective	51
Chapter 16	Echo	53

Chapter 17	Breathing through your feet	56
Chapter 18	Real courage	59
Chapter 19	Inspection	62
Chapter 20	Work and rest	75
Part 2 summary		78

PART 3 LEADING EVERY DAY: THE BASICS — 83

Chapter 21	Curiosity	85
Chapter 22	Process, not place	88
Chapter 23	Smiling	92
Chapter 24	Saying thank you	95
Chapter 25	Questions	98
Chapter 26	Visits	101
Chapter 27	Feedback	104
Chapter 28	Next steps	107
Chapter 29	The gift of helping others to cross stepping stones	110
Chapter 30	The importance of preparation	113
Chapter 31	Meetings	116
Chapter 32	Reading	122
Chapter 33	Carrying on	125
Chapter 34	Restart	128
Chapter 35	Moments that give perspective	132
Part 3 summary		134

PART 4 LEADING EVERY DAY: MINDSET AND CULTURE — 139

Chapter 36	The importance of goals	141
Chapter 37	Little things that mean a lot	143
Chapter 38	Slowly building trust	145
Chapter 39	Positive narratives	148

Chapter 40	Quiet ambition	151
Chapter 41	The misconception of strong leadership	154
Chapter 42	Benches	158
Chapter 43	The self-employed mindset	161
Chapter 44	Taking measured risks	164
Chapter 45	The pitfall of the self-employed mindset	167
Chapter 46	Threads	170
Chapter 47	Tuning forks	173
Chapter 48	Pipelines	176
Chapter 49	Working sideways across schools	180
Part 4 summary		185

Conclusion	189
Afterword	192
References	198
Additional resources	200
Index	207

Meet the author

Neil Renton is the headteacher of a large comprehensive secondary school with over 2100 pupils in North Yorkshire. An experienced senior leader, he was appointed to headship just before the pandemic.

Acknowledgements

Twenty years ago, I wrote an article on the use of electronic whiteboards in schools. My wife read this and said, '*possibly one of the most boring things I have ever read*'. I would like to thank her for helping me become a better writer, I hope. She has persevered and pointed me gently in the direction of improvement. I thank her for her ability to perceive things from every angle and temper my judgement, making me a better leader. Her endless support, encouragement and patience made a project like this achievable. I would like to thank her for listening to me read sections aloud before reading the many drafts.

I thank Kirstie Moat, Tim Milburn, David Jones, Angela Toulson, Per Haglund and Mick Walker for also reading drafts and for pointing me in the right direction. Thank you also to Gemma Quarmby, Matthew Partington, Emma Meadus and Rob Higgins for their insights into leadership.

I am unapologetically an observer of people, and I would like to thank all the individuals in this book who have brought texture to my thinking about leadership. The team of staff where I work dedicate themselves to the culture of our school, helping each other and serving the incredible children in our care.

I have led the school with Kirstie at my side now for several years. She is an incredible co-pilot and inspires me to be a better leader every day, simply by being herself. Kirstie stress-tests my reasoning and displays the deepest empathy, honesty and commitment I have ever seen. Tim and the rest of my senior team, with the support of Angela, deserve a special mention. I learn, laugh and lead with them every day and embrace a culture that is so positive and proactive – thank you.

For every headteacher and leader that I have worked for, I have studied and tried to model your habits, techniques and styles that work for me. Thank you to Ian MacNaughton, Gillian James, Mark Tweedle, Mike Cook, Stephen Gregson and Richard Sheriff for every lesson you gave me, even though you didn't know you were teaching me. Stepping up to headship was an opportunity given to me by Richard Sheriff and he has been a role model, mentor and professional friend to me. He put trust and belief in me, and that is the most powerful lesson about leadership.

I hope you take from this book an important lesson. Leadership is not a fixed quality that only some people are able to do. It takes focus and energy and is a process of gradual improvement that anyone can do. Whatever the challenges that you will inevitably face, you have what it takes to be the very best leader. Stay positive and remember that, on the whole, they are all good days.

Endorsements

Something happens when you step from being a senior leader to being appointed as headteacher. Everyone tells you it will feel different, but no one can quite explain how. Neil Renton's book does just that. From its first sentence, it presents the most authentic and powerfully articulated account of the shift that happens inside us as we take on the mantle of head or principal. I like the book's mixture of candour, values and practical insights. I like its lack of misty-eyed sentimentalism. I like the way it focuses on the details of headship – the interactions with staff, the decision-making process, the skills involved in communicating with clarity and openness. This is no checklist of tricks and gimmicks. It's a reassuringly honest yet optimistic reminder of the day-to-day reality of one of society's most important roles: being a headteacher. I thoroughly recommend it.

Geoff Barton
General Secretary, Association of School and College Leaders (ASCL)

Leading a school for the first time is a little bit like setting off to sea on an inaugural voyage as the captain of a ship. Few leadership roles give you the privilege to set the course and take daily responsibility for the lives, welfare, and success of so many souls.

Neil Renton has just been on that journey and has used his sharp and curious mind to continually reflect on the experience and the lessons learned along the way. For anyone aspiring to lead, or who has recently started out on their own leadership voyage, this is an invaluable read that will help counter some of the negative stereotypes that exist about those who lead our schools.

You won't find action plans, spreadsheets or checklists of how to make a school 'outstanding' in New School Leader: What Now? *What you will find are insights into establishing the right culture and key lessons about what really matters when you come to leading a school.*

I hope this book will encourage many more principled, generous, and passionate leaders to set out to sea.

**Richard Sheriff OBE
CEO of the Red Kite Learning Trust
ASCL past president**

Introduction

This is the one book that I looked for when I became a headteacher that I couldn't find. You hear the exciting news *'we would like to offer you the job'*, but then you have that awful feeling of *'what do I do now?'*.

This book answers that very question with simple lessons that will help you to navigate, in Part 1, that nagging feeling of self-doubt all leaders face. In Part 2, I turn to lessons about the challenges that you will inevitably face. Part 3 addresses the very basics of leading every day. Finally, Part 4 explores setting your own mindset and the culture of your school.

This book is based on how I answered the question *'what now?'*. It tells my story about how I learnt to lead, as a new headteacher, through a pandemic, an Ofsted inspection and the everyday running of one of the largest comprehensive state schools in the UK.

In the context of a crisis of recruitment for teachers and headteachers leaving the profession after five years or so, I hope that this book helps you to find answers to *New School Leader: What Now?* Schools need leaders like you. Leaders who embrace the challenges of leading and who take those gradual, incremental steps of learning to lead.

Neil Renton, 2023

Part 1
NAVIGATING DOUBT

Chapter 1

LEARNING TO CARRY THE WEIGHT

Today the school felt different. On a bitterly cold December day, the sun flooded the main corridor with light. I walked towards the staffroom, standing slightly taller, moving with a little more confidence, and all my senses felt alive.

I had been striving to be a headteacher for the last ten years, and today I walked down the corridor having achieved that goal. The CEO had offered me the position late on the previous Thursday evening, after two gruelling days of interviews. I spent Friday in a daze before escaping with my wife and son to Newcastle to celebrate. I needed to take some time to think about the opportunity I had been given. I needed to take a deep breath before getting back to work.

As I walked along the corridor, the hum of the school seemed sharper, the windows brighter and the air clearer. I felt more responsible. I felt pride. Then, I really felt it. The weight made me feel it. A very heavy weight. I imagined all the interactions in the school, the number of staff, the number of parents, the previous headteachers, our culture, the building, the duties and the roles, and I took another deep breath. A wise, long-established and highly respected teacher laughed with me before the interview and said that he '*wouldn't want this job for all the tea in China*'. I thought of him now and smiled. The weight didn't frighten me. I could just about hold it, but I needed to toughen up.

As a child I'd got used to my parents saying to me '*son, if you carry a calf every day of your life, you can carry a cow*'. I knew I would get used to the weight. I needed to give it some time. Nothing really prepared me, though, for that unique and almost lonely feeling of finally stepping up to that position. I thought I had experienced it in previous senior positions, but not until I took on headship did I fully feel the weight. Day by day, decision after decision, interaction after interaction, I became accustomed to that responsibility. I slowly became a headteacher by listening to others, learning from my mistakes, reflecting on my performance and striving to be better. The CEO gifted me the ultimate leadership role when he appointed me, but that was only the beginning of learning to lead.

It took time to become comfortable with the weight. When you take on a leadership position, you must draw on everything you have experienced, learnt and observed. Leadership is a privilege and as a new school leader asking yourself *'what now?'*, you must simply reflect, refine, practise and develop so you can carry the weight.

> *When awarded the privilege of the ultimate leadership position, recognise that this is only the beginning of learning to lead.*

REFLECTION QUESTION

What role models and experiences of leading can you draw upon to help you carry the weight?

TASKS

1. List all the elements of your new role that you must carry and that feel heavy.
2. Divide these into goals and expectations, people, teams and other pressures.
3. For each area, note the strategies that you could take to help you carry the weight of responsibility.

Chapter 2
THE IMPORTANCE OF ALLIES

I like it when my closest colleagues catch a word, offer advice, provide critical feedback or look at me with shared understanding. Their presence gives me confidence and their feedback fosters the humility needed as a leader to always develop.

I look out to the school hall with 400 parents sitting waiting for me to speak. The moment before I start, my mind blanks, fear, as if I am about to choke. A simple strategy that I have learnt to rescue myself from my potential demise is to write the first sentence I am going to say on a piece of paper in front of me as a prompt. However, my closest allies are my biggest help during high-stakes speeches. The knowledge that they are present calms my mind, making it feel as though I am talking with people I trust.

On the second day of the interview for the position of headteacher, one of the selection tasks involved candidates talking with all staff about why they applied for the job. Waiting outside the room, knowing that 150 staff were standing in the round, prepared and ready to observe this stressful event, I took the deepest breaths. This helped but wasn't enough. With a racing mind and a strong desire to run away, I talked with two of my closest allies, one who had also applied for the job and the other, our boss. We smiled and laughed about how we felt. My closest allies know how to use humour. Humour helps navigate the most challenging of circumstances and seems to present itself when people truly understand the reality of a situation.

I value humility in my colleagues – the ability to reflect, receive feedback and honestly evaluate their own performance. Those colleagues often use good humour – almost a sign of their advanced social skills. My closest allies have a bucket full of humility that inspires me to be humble. I want them to critique me and give me feedback so I can be the best that I can. One of my closest allies once tried to tidy my curly hair. I didn't like this, but his words on how to set expectations, stand tall and *'give it some welly'* pushed me forward.

Erving Goffman (1959) wrote about the presentation of self in everyday life – how individuals construct meaning through daily social interaction with others. As leaders, we all learn to present ourselves as if we are on a stage – notebooks in our hands, fountain pens, suits and smart offices as our props. We learn to play roles and find it difficult when we experience role conflict – for example, buying cat food, toilet roll, a bottle of wine and flowers for your wife carries a certain level of awkwardness when a pupil serves you at the till. It is, however, never awkward with my closest allies. They are close to me and make me feel confident to be my real self. Close allies give confidence, and their feedback can refresh your humility so you can develop.

Take confidence from your closest allies to be your true self. Let their feedback refresh your humility so you can develop.

REFLECTION QUESTION

What can you learn from the honest feedback of your closest allies as you step into your new role?

TASKS

1. Identify your closest allies.
2. Imagine each one of them sitting in a row giving you detailed feedback. What do they say?
3. Be humble, ask them directly.
4. List the feedback that gives you confidence, followed by what they think you need to do differently.

Chapter 3
WORKING WITHOUT PRAISE

Shame and pride seem to be very powerful emotions. Shame hinges on a negative evaluation of yourself – a painful feeling of worthlessness – and pride, the reverse – a deeply satisfying feeling about your achievements. Shaming and praising have wildly different effects on an individual's self-worth. We see relationships with excessive levels of shaming as pernicious. Yet, we also see excessive levels of praise as unrealistic, delusional and misconceived.

Shame and pride are both important in how you come to understand your own performance. A little bit of shame or embarrassment teaches you humility. It helps you, at that point of failure, to form a more accurate interpretation of how effective you have been. Pride, based on praise for worthy achievement, can also be part of an accurate interpretation of the self.

Imagine two children on a seesaw, one called *Shame* and the other *Pride*, one goes up, one goes down and vice versa. In their play, *Shame* and *Pride* find that perfect spot of balance. They look at each other, smiling, before one or the other makes the next move. Being a new leader feels a bit like being on a seesaw. On rare occasions, we can find that moment when *Pride* looks directly in the eye of *Shame* on the seesaw.

Leaders sometimes say that '*leadership is lonely*'. This is especially true, regarding praise. Successful colleagues progress through organisations experiencing lots of praise. They gain status, get bigger offices and receive lots of praise. When you become a leader, the lines of authentic praise simply dry up. Yes, you may receive positive feedback from staff, but you always question whether that is because of you or the role that you hold. In contrast, shame, self-doubt, imposter syndrome and negative thoughts become much stronger when you lead.

I am learning to be much more confident and realise that the sacrifice of leadership is that I work with less praise. And in doing so, I have decided to get off the seesaw. Instead, I am focusing on others finding their balance on the seesaw and giving authentic praise.

> *Be comfortable about working with less praise.*

REFLECTION QUESTION

How does working with less praise impact on you as a new school leader?

TASKS

1. Note all the things that you are proud of in your work as a leader.
2. Next, note your negative thoughts, areas where you feel like an imposter in your role, areas of doubt and negative perceptions you hold of yourself.
3. Reassure yourself that the first list contains impact, and the second list has little value, other than to derail you.
4. Shift your focus to praising others well.

Chapter 4
PLAIN SPEAKING

I watch leaders during meetings. Headteachers seem so confident when they speak. They talk with ease in front of others and know exactly what to say. I am not like that. Sometimes the flow of my speech breaks and my thoughts run quicker than the movement of my mouth. When a situation overwhelms me, my speech is breathless and anxious. I wonder how others speak with such confidence and ease.

When Basil Bernstein (1964) studied speech codes in the East End of London and developed the concepts of *elaborate* and *restricted* speech codes, he defined something that I struggle with in a crowded room. The *elaborate* code of formal communication, syntactic completeness and in-depth expression seems just out of my reach. The *restricted code* of shortened speech, simplistic sentence structures, unfinished sentences and sometimes non-standard grammar seem to be more firmly in my hand. I am comfortable with an *elaborate code* when I pick up a pen or write a letter, but I struggle to unlock and speak that code when I open my mouth. I find the spoken craft far harder than the written form.

I overcome this barrier when I speak in front of others with a few simple techniques. Significant speeches are much easier. You can plan these in advance, but it is the unplanned world of meetings, briefings and everyday interactions that demands a quicker, more spontaneous response. I hold in my mind a simple structure I can hang my words upon: describe the wider problem, the immediate problem and then the proposed solution. Alternatively, I make two points – firstly, secondly – and then end with the underlying central point. I remind myself that listening is far more important than speaking, anyway. I need to understand as much as possible about the people I lead, their thoughts and their ideas.

One of the most useful strategies is not to avoid speech, but to let others do far more of it. I ask question after question to help me understand. Talking with a pre-planned structure and asking questions, mainly *'why?'*, helps to hide my affiliation with the *restricted code*.

My colleagues in the Design Faculty had worked together on innovations to make a difference in the pandemic, developing a prototype visor using a laser cutter before manufacturing 1000 visors in a week to help with a shortage of personal protective equipment for health professionals. A journalist from the *Guardian* had picked up on this story and asked for an interview. I was typically apprehensive and nervous about the spoken word. But this was a remarkable effort, and all I needed to do was explain what they had achieved. And I think this is where the most important point about the spoken word needs to be made – speak plainly.

When faced with saying something important, I trust my understanding and try to speak plainly. Speaking plainly means capturing the essential point that I need to make. When the journalist asked me why the teachers were making PPE, I paused and said, '*I think it comes from an overwhelming desire from our teachers and staff, who believe in public service, to make a difference*'. These are not the most elaborate words, but they capture the meaning. I am learning to be confident in my own plain speaking.

Find the communication style that fits with you as a leader – for me, that is plain speaking.

REFLECTION QUESTION

What communication style plays to your natural strength as a leader?

TASKS

1. List all the different scenarios where you must speak publicly in your role.
2. For each scenario, write an underlying structure for what you might say. This could be three points or a general point, followed by an example, before a call to action.

Chapter 5

SPEAKING FROM THE HEART

When I spoke to the entire staff team before we closed the school at the start of the first lockdown, it was important that I spoke from my heart. Within 48 hours, we had said our rushed goodbyes to Year 11 and Year 13. Staff knew that this would be the end for a while.

There would be over 150 staff, standing in the round, looking to me for leadership and a sense of meaning in the most uncertain of times. As I moved through each bullet point on my list, I reached the point where it was time to speak from the heart. I needed to explain what the closure of school meant to me, how I felt about our team, how they pulled together in recent weeks, the pride that I felt and the sorrow of what was ahead. I knew I was speaking from my heart, no need for bullet points, with emotion in my voice; the room fell silent.

Sometimes when you are leading and speaking from the front, you catch moments where you are looking in upon your own self – almost like a view from above, a second lens. I had that feeling. It was so quiet I could only hear the echo of my voice. I could see some staff with tears in their eyes, and this compelled me to speak even more freely. As I brought my words to a close, the staff broke into an applause that seemed to last for a very long time. They weren't clapping me, they were applauding the culture of our school and the togetherness of the situation.

You learn a lot in the most difficult of times and this experience showed me that speaking from the heart, showing some emotion and humility as a leader, unites people. Public speakers use all kinds of strategies to engage the audience, telling stories and using different vocal techniques. Speaking from the heart, though, when faced with the most challenging of circumstances, and showing your vulnerability as a leader simply seem the right things to do.

Speaking from the heart points me to important values and emotions. I speak of the pride that I have in others, pride in how people care for children and pride in our whole organisation. I speak of privilege and honour, the privilege that I have to lead this team and how honoured I am to work with them. The value of serving others and trying to make a difference.

Speaking from the heart is a vulnerability for a leader. You reveal the essence of who you are. This is not who you are in that moment, but who you have become through your upbringing, education and adult experience. You lay bare your core values, how you see others, what they mean to you and ultimately what defines you as a leader. Speaking from the heart is deeply personal.

My privacy is important to me, but I know that when you lead a large organisation, you give of yourself to others. Speaking from the heart, to me, is a gift that I can give my team in times of crisis. It shows bravery, humility and brings people together through words that show kindness, understanding and empathy. However much you may battle with demons of shyness or introversion as a new leader, there will be a time where you must speak from the heart.

> *Recognise the powerful impact of speaking from the heart and show vulnerability as a leader.*

REFLECTION QUESTION

Why is speaking from the heart, at an appropriate time, such an effective communication strategy?

TASKS

1. Consider when, in previous roles, you have spoken from the heart.
2. What was the impact?
3. When is it appropriate to do this?

Chapter 6
DECISIONS

I walked into the headteacher's office when I was working as an assistant headteacher. My headteacher sat in his large leather-bound chair and turned to greet me. I had just had a difficult meeting with a member of staff who had been critical of the decision that I had made to change the end-of-term reports. The school were using pre-written comment banks for targets for pupils. I felt that the comments were generic and applicable to all children. I wanted the teachers to provide more direction and give children specific feedback about what they needed to do to improve. These would be unique to each child. I took the decision to remove the meaningless targets from the reports and ask teachers to issue specific targets to children in their classes – very simple.

My headteacher acted as my counsel whilst I was trying to backtrack from the decision I had made. I started describing my decision as *'bad'* and argued against my own view from the perspective of my disgruntled colleague. My headteacher explained that I shouldn't do this. I had made the decision with all the information available to me. I shouldn't look back now. It was the right decision. I acted with conviction.

I now sit in the headteacher's office as the headteacher and think back to that moment. The decision I had just made was now, without a doubt, poor. I acted on the information available to me, but I had missed something. I had suspended a child for their behaviour after a brief conversation with an assistant headteacher who needed a quick decision. The teacher was in a heightened state, and I supported his decision too quickly. I failed to take my time to go through the case, ask questions and fully understand the circumstances.

Now, as the situation had calmed and all the information had come to light about provocation and who had done what, the decision to suspend looked off the mark. Frustrated, it was all too easy to project blame onto the teacher for *'not telling me all the facts'*. But I made the decision, too quickly, and without asking enough questions.

Leaders make hundreds of judgements and decisions. Making a poor decision, from time to time, serves as a powerful reminder of what we need to do to make decisions that we can comfortably live with.

We must fully prepare if we are going to make an effective decision. When you cook a meal, build a wall or bake a cake, you gather all the ingredients, tools and materials together before you start. Decision-making is just the same, but you must gather *all the information* you need. Information alone, however, is not nearly enough. It needs to be the right information, from colleagues you trust. To make an effective judgement, the information must be honest, comprehensive, valid and reliable.

You must challenge and explore the information. You should ask question after question from many perspectives – why is this the best next step, what will happen if you don't act, what are the other options? Then ask, *'why am I making this decision?'* and *'what are the unintended consequences if I decide this or that?'*.

When I make hard decisions, I remind myself that I need to exercise all my previous experience, knowledge and expertise. I remind myself to trust this experience, combined with my values, to make the right call. This, however, is still not enough. Bias creeps over leaders, like ivy on a wall. Although you must always make the final decision, checking for your bias helps you to make a better judgement. I express my thinking with a trusted member of my leadership team to see if bias has got the better of me. Even expressing my thinking aloud to myself can help me see flaws in my reasoning.

The final thought before I make the last call is to remind myself that decisions can have their own momentum; some are quick and some are slow. Sometimes it is better to pause and let the situation develop. Sometimes people expect you to be quick. The beauty of leadership is that, most of the time, you can put a harness around the force that drives the need for the decision. You can steer this force and set it in the right direction.

I look back now to the counsel I received in the headteacher's office and reflect on the complexity of decision-making. Decision-making involves the interplay of so many factors and this makes it a gruelling task. It is all too easy to look back and be angry with others or yourself about the decisions you made. Decision-making needs confidence and conviction. It is a thorny process that new leaders need to respect and refine.

> *Making poor decisions is a powerful reminder to think about how you make decisions – gather all the right information, challenge this, draw on your experience and check your bias.*

REFLECTION **QUESTION**

What processes do you follow to make a good decision?

TASKS

1. Identify the worst and best decisions that you have ever made as a leader.
2. Explain the interplay of different factors in your reasoning that led to the worst and best decisions.
3. Why do you have more conviction in some decisions than others?

Chapter 7
U-TURNS

I remember driving to the Lake District from Yorkshire for a Christmas holiday with family. We faced the seemingly endless task of packing the car and getting everyone finally out of the house. After I locked the house door, with a final double check to confirm it was really locked, I jumped in the car and asked, *'have we got everything?'*. I failed to ask the specific *'is everything turned off'*, but ask the general, *'have we got everything?'*. The answer, of course, *'yes, think so'* reverberates around the car.

Many hours later, my daughter approaches me – apprehensive, sheepish and tentative. *'Dad, you know the new set of candles I bought? I think I left them burning in my bedroom.'* And there begins my relationship with U-turns. New information comes to light, you need to take responsibility and act. It was time to drive back home on Christmas Eve to blow the candles out.

U-turns surround us in politics and education. The pandemic saw more U-turns than we care to remember – no free school meal vouchers during the holiday, free school meal vouchers continue, all primary children return to school, no, they can't, exam algorithms are robust, no, they are not, no masks, masks on, masks off, etc.

There is something about the drama of a U-turn, the fall from grace, that grabs our attention, creating a narrative of fear and shame around U-turns. I disagree with this view and believe that, *very occasionally*, U-turns are important in leadership. The feeling before a U-turn, that sinking feeling or moment of clarity, represents a moment of motivation. It serves you with an opportunity to put something right.

The last day of term for Year 11 often conjures fear in school leaders. I have heard stories of a headteacher's door being removed, chickens being released, fire alarms going off, school gates being padlocked so no one can get in, fish left in lockers, an endless list of possibilities. No one wants this. In the year the government had cancelled exams, our pupils faced a week of final assessments before they finished for the summer. They were to have their last assessment on Friday morning, then an afternoon of lessons before leaving school. The routine of leavers' assemblies was cancelled as we were avoiding large group gatherings. All our normal routines were being blown away due to the pandemic. In short, lots of opportunity for things to go wrong.

On Thursday morning, a member of my senior leadership team raised his concern about how challenging it was going to be to teach Year 11 on Friday afternoon after such a pressured final week of assessments. *'But that isn't our culture, surely we can engage our pupils in lessons on the final afternoon'*, I challenged. I wasn't for moving; the pupils should stay for the day, spending time together and saying farewell to their classes. Then the moment of doubt started as another colleague casually mentioned a rumour that someone was going to *'do something'* and release our school chickens. I asked for the chickens to be secured, and that gave me a moment of reprieve from my doubt. A further conversation with a colleague confirmed that holding our position was the right thing to do. Then it rained, and rained; wet break and wet lunch. Children cooped up all day. You could feel the pressure building.

On Friday morning, the same theme came up, but the team had gone away and forged a plan. They were talking about how they could increase supervision. They charged their walkie-talkies – they were meeting my expectation that we would finish the day at the normal time. The rain continued and our new build had sprung a leak. The coiled spring of finishing school and the tension of the final assessment made me feel uneasy. I left the meeting and knew that I needed to ask, *'Should I U-turn, allow an earlier finish, recognise the unique experience the pupils have faced in the pandemic and release them at lunch?'* I had that U-turn feeling. The circumstances had changed. I U-turned.

I think that when new information comes to light, when colleagues are doing as you ask even when they don't agree, and when you can see that only you are able to address the situation, then make the U-turn. Seek the advice of colleagues, but then make your own decision with confidence. Avoid picking over what you have done and have the courage to stand by your decision.

Have the courage to U-turn when new information comes to light.

REFLECTION QUESTION

Should leaders very rarely U-turn?

TASKS

1. Consider a decision you made that, in hindsight, you wished you had U-turned.
2. What stopped you?
3. What steps can you take to stop picking over decisions that you have made?

Chapter 8
KOPFKINO

'What are you thinking about?' Nothing, I answer. *'Just playing something out in my head.' Kopfkino* – the German word for a cinema in your head.

Spending time in my *Kopfkino* is an important part of being a new leader, and it takes different forms. You can watch a scenario again and see how it might have looked if you had done something differently. Alternatively, you can jump to the future and watch how things might play out.

We all have places we like to be when we drift into or purposefully enter our *Kopfkino*. I like to switch mine on a few hours into a long train or car journey. Something about the movement allows me to stride into the imagined. Other times, I enjoy lying on my back and looking up at the clouds. The feel of grass at my fingertips, the sound of birds and the smell of summer. Thoughts and ideas drift across my mind and *Kopfkino* lets me press play and watch the past, present or future. Leaders, however, are not often afforded the pleasure of their favourite place and must quickly switch on their *Kopfkino* at work.

When a colleague suggests a new idea at pace in a meeting, you need to play out what might happen if you were to enact their proposal. I try to let my *Kopfkino* show this with the *intended consequences* and then replay with the potential *unintended consequences*. If the ending of the show of *unintended consequences* is not so great, it is time to explore a different idea.

At interviews, I sometimes switch on my *Kopfkino* and watch the teacher in a future class, in a meeting, with a parent and when facing challenges. *Kopfkino* draws on everything they said in the day, the inputs, and pieces together a film for me to watch.

When I face a tough conversation, I often spend some time before in *Kopfkino*. I try to watch the story unfold in all manifestations and think about how I might react. I then rewind and take the story in its new direction. *Kopfkino* allows me to shift perspective and watch the film from someone else's eyes. I can play it from my lens, their lens, or jump to someone looking into the scene. You can change the perspective of the onlooker to different role models or colleagues. I watch the story again and think about how the scenario might now unfold if I were them.

Sometimes *Kopfkino* takes me far away into the future. There is something about seeing the early stages of a building project in school, or when decorating at home, that takes me into my *Kopfkino* of dreams, hopes and aspirations. What might the school look like in the future? What will colleagues be doing? *Kopfkino* provides a view.

When things are difficult or when I am trying to achieve something significant, I try to let my *Kopfkino* play out the success. I watch this on repeat in the hope that a real-life script will form with a positive narrative that I just need to follow.

Whilst *Kopfkino* seems to exist without limits, it is not without flaws. My *Kopfkino* sometimes just cannot grasp the extent to which all things are contingent. However much I try to play things out, I have learnt that it often misses out on an important scene. I am reminded that my *Kopfkino* does this when someone says, '*we didn't see that coming*'.

Kopfkino can get carried away with itself and so is not always a reliable oracle. Our own prejudices, fears, habits often infect our

Kopfkino with over-emotional or sensationalist ideas. We are not our most reliable narrator.

I have learnt, however, to let others help me see more. '*You look like you are deep in thought, Neil?*' said Angela, my PA. '*Oh no, I was just working something out.*' I explain this to her and ask, '*what do you think will happen?*' '*Is it a good idea?*' Angela will spot something that I haven't seen and then say, '*think about it*'. I return to my *Kopfkino* to watch again.

Kopfkino plays an important role for new leaders. It lets you watch potential scenarios and see probable outcomes from the eyes of others. We would be wise to not spend all our time in it, though, as the real world is always much more authentic and reliant on the actions of others. And it is possible to let the cinema in our heads run away with itself, and create unnecessary panic or stress.

> *Spend some time in the cinema in your head to play out plausible scenarios and see potential outcomes from the eyes of others.*

REFLECTION QUESTION

What role can *Kopfkino* play for you as a new school leader?

TASKS

1. Consider a change that you would like to bring about and visualise what this will look like.
2. Play out the change now in your *Kopfkino* with the unintended consequence.
3. Play out the change again from the perspective of others in as many scenarios as you can imagine.
4. Remind yourself that your *Kopfkino* may not be accurate and the real world is just that – real.

Chapter 9

FORGETTING AND REMEMBERING

I look at my scribbled writing in my notebook. I can't quite make out what I have written. Infuriated, I try my best to remember. It must have been important. I only write important things in my notebook. I need to remember. I pace around my office to entice the entry back to the forefront of my mind. That still doesn't work. I look at my scribble again with intensity and take out a blank piece of paper. I try to repeat the pen strokes to see if that triggers anything. Finally, I give up. If it were important, I would remember.

Experience tells me I will remember; maybe when I just arrive home or in the early hours of the morning. Should new leaders worry, however, about forgetting?

It is five days into the holiday, and I am forgetting much of what has happened in the last term, forgetting the emails that have arrived that I have simply flagged and forgetting all the things on my to-do list. I am determined to rest, so I must forget.

As the days pass, I know that all those experiences, ideas and interactions are whirring around, and occasionally cropping up in my mind. Some of them pass through my mind like a quick text message, others linger, and I ponder before letting them pass. The memory of the past few months gradually takes shape, an interpretation of my lived experience. A new lens that is entirely my own and a lens that will soften and evolve over time.

The idea of motivated forgetting seems to make sense, a process that allows us to forget unwanted memories. Undoubtedly, we need to forget much of what we experience as leaders, but just how much should we forget and how much should we remember?

Forgetting is important for self-preservation for leaders, especially when we lead through the inevitable challenges we face, but this should not be at the expense of progress and positive change. We should worry about forgetting if it leads to inaction. There is always learning in failings, and we must avoid allowing forgetting to get in the way. We need to remember to change the right things that make a difference.

I walk to school in the morning, and those previously illegible words in my notebook become clearer. That was it, I now know what I need to do. Interestingly, my memory has developed as a headteacher. I hear lots of information, read lots of reports and experience many interactions that repeat the same point. Maybe this helps me remember.

But should I worry about *motivated forgetting*? Yes. New leaders face tough challenges that it may be helpful to forget – however, they must identify the real issue to address, only then can they affect change.

> *Forgetting is important but should not be at the expense of addressing tough challenges and creating positive change.*

REFLECTION QUESTION

How much should we forget and how much should we remember as a new school leader?

> **TASKS**
>
> 1. Consider a situation that you have dealt with where a genuine failing has taken place but where you didn't effectively follow this up.
> 2. What steps could you have taken to bring about positive change?

Chapter 10
VISIBILITY

Three words contain an important lesson: *'who are you?'* I don't hear these words very often, but when I do, they challenge me to think about my visibility. The first time I heard them from a pupil, it may have been a joke, but it filled me with embarrassment. I blushed. The second time I heard them from a visitor, and it made me smile. They simply didn't know, and we laughed together, quickly softening how awkward interactions sometimes feel. The third time, I heard them in defence as I told a pupil off. The words *'who are you?'* hit me. I thought, *'I try to be everywhere. How can you not know who I am?'*

I am learning to reframe my thinking about visibility more positively. There are over 2100 pupils in our school, almost 4000 parents, and many wider connections. It is perfectly logical that someone might not know who I am, and it is perfectly acceptable to think that I may need to make myself more visible. When I hear *'who are you?'* I challenge myself to be humble, doubling my efforts to be more visible.

In the day-to-day business of leadership, we often say *'yes'*, our diaries fill, and we appear to hide away in endless meetings. Our visibility diminishes despite feeling busy. Never fully achieved, visibility takes focus. And when you make this a focus, you remove the embarrassment of being asked, *'who are you?'*

Two strategies help me to keep visible. First, thinking about where I place myself. Even when my diary is full, there are places in school where pupils see me. If I stand at the front of the school at the start and the end of the day, I can welcome pupils to school. If I stand at the front of the dinner queue, I can see many children before their lunch. If I walk at break time, I can select a route to maximise visibility. If I stand up straight and walk tall, I can increase my visibility.

Second, saying *'yes'* to things that make me visible. If someone asks me to watch something, take part in an interview, write for a local newspaper or just say a few words, I say *'yes'*.

There is, however, more to visibility than simply being seen. It is easy to fall into a silent trap of distraction, with after-thoughts of meetings and things you need to get done that cloud your presence. But preoccupation kills visibility. When I leave my office, I try to go beyond being simply seen. I say hello, ask *'how are you?'*, smile and connect.

Make visibility a focus.

REFLECTION QUESTION

How visible are you as a new school leader?

TASKS

1. What steps can you take to increase your visibility?
2. How can you approach visibility with intentionality?

Chapter 11
ASKING FOR HELP

I sit back in my chair at my desk. I draw breath and then quickly close my lips tight, releasing a heavy breath out of my nose. I place my pen on my desk. Now, staring into space, I admit to myself that I am stuck. Trying again to find the answer, I cup my chin with my hand. I blink, frown, grimace and shake my head. This doesn't make a difference. I remain stuck.

New leaders easily fall into the trap of thinking that they need to know everything and solve every problem. You have taken on the role of leading and because you are at the front, you must know what to do. You become used to being asked questions and helping others. You convince yourself that you know the answer and that your answer is correct. I call this mindset the *arrogance-veil trap*. New leaders would be wise to shield themselves from this by unveiling the potential solutions by simply asking for help.

It takes humility and vulnerability to ask for help. A different way of thinking, counter to the *'follow my leader, leader, leader'* associated with the *arrogance-veil trap*. Rather than simply *'follow my leader'*, a crucial leadership skill is *identification*. This is the ability to see and select the flaws and cracks within the school and then ask, *'who is best placed to help me solve this problem?'*

When new leaders escape the thinking of the *arrogance-veil trap* to the liminal space of seeking help, they unlock potential answers and solutions. There are three simple strategies to help when you are stuck. These take you far beyond your own knowledge and expertise.

Share the problem. By explaining to others *'I'm struggling with this'*, you are inviting them to think, innovate and contribute a solution. In recent weeks, I have been asking my leadership team to think about something that I am stuck with and then revisiting this after they have had time to reflect, talk with others and develop solutions. Invariably, we unlock potential solutions or nudge nearer to the answer. There is something deeply motivational in inviting others to help, especially when they then feel part of putting something right.

Use and build networks. Sometimes the flaw or crack that you have identified needs understanding through the lens of experts outside of your school. Leaders in other schools will have likely faced a similar problem and have expertise in an area you simply don't. You must be open and humble about what they might see or say; they can play a vital role in effecting change. New leaders asking *'what now?'* would be wise to build relationships with many leaders – new, experienced or retired – to help them get unstuck.

Have a mentor. Richard, the CEO of our Multi-Academy Trust, has an office a ten-minute walk from our school. We have an allocated time, once a fortnight, where I step outside of school and visit him. When we meet, we focus on one or two areas where I am stuck. I explain the problem and then what I think is the solution. He often helps me think this through by drawing on a giant whiteboard on his wall, trying to show different areas to think about. As a mentor, he creates a space where ideas spark more ideas. Having someone you trust who has faced many similar problems before and who has the wisdom to help *you* select the most effective path is vital for new leaders.

That moment when you feel entirely stuck is an important junction for a leader. Turning to others rather than falling into the *arrogance-veil trap* takes humility and recognition that you can't do everything or know all the answers. There is much greater power in working with others than in trying to solve the problem alone. People want to help and support new leaders. Simply learn to spot when you need to ask.

Recognise when you need to ask for help and avoid the arrogance-veil trap. Share the problem, use and build networks, and make sure you have a trusted mentor.

REFLECTION QUESTION

What role does humility and vulnerability play in effective leadership?

TASKS

1. List the current flaws and cracks where you are stuck.
2. Share the problem with colleagues and give them time to come up with potential answers.
3. Invite someone from your network to help you solve the same problem.
4. Explore all the potential solutions with your mentor.

Part 1
SUMMARY

Doubt seems like an inevitable experience when taking on a new leadership role. Its presence can question you to the core and make you feel out of your depth. However, day by day the weight of responsibility becomes easier to carry with the support of close allies and getting used to working with less praise.

With good old plain speaking and learning to communicate honestly you gain confidence in your decision-making. The cinema in your head, *Kopfkino*, can then help you to find your way through challenging issues, along with humility, when new information comes to light, to U-turn. Forgetting is also an important part of self-preservation for new leaders, but not so that you ignore what needs to change. And when someone doesn't know who you are, don't panic. Simply redouble your efforts to be seen.

One of the most effect ways to cope with doubt is to simply ask for help. Learn quickly to recognise when you need to lean on others.

Part of navigating doubt is also about having the right mindset, which we will explore in Part 4 on mindsets and culture. But the experience of navigating challenges and learning the basics of leading every day comes first. Next, we turn to *'what now?'* when staring in the face of challenge. Before we do, Gemma Quarmby, headteacher at Whitkirk Primary, reminds us of the importance of visibility and asking for help when navigating doubt.

Part 1 Case study
Gemma Quarmby on navigating doubt

Name	Gemma Quarmby
Setting	Whitkirk Primary School, Red Kite Learning Trust, Leeds – primary school of 400 pupils
Role	Headteacher
If you could give two pieces of advice to a new school leader to help them navigate doubt, what would you say?	Believe in yourself as others clearly do. There is a reason you're in the position that you're in today. Your hard work, your commitment and your talents have been recognised during what is likely to have been a rigorous process and you have been selected as the best person for the job. You may not and will not know everything, but if you did, would the role be so rewarding, would it be the desired next step in your career? I imagine not. Embrace the challenge, be open-minded and seek support from a mentor or colleagues in a similar role. Asking for help or support is not a sign of weakness, it's a strength and shows your commitment and drive to further develop – you will be amazed at how many people want to help you. Utilise the team and the people around you. Leadership shouldn't be lonely and there's no way that success in a school can be achieved single-handedly. Invest time in getting to know each person within your team individually. This will help you find out their strengths and their areas for development, how they work best as part of a team, and allow you to really connect with them to ensure that they feel valued.

→

What is the most important leadership book to you?	Munby, S (2019) *Imperfect Leadership: A Book for Leaders Who Know They Don't Know It All*. Carmarthen: Crown House Publishing.
Why is this book important?	It is practical, relatable and honest with a focus on leading with a moral purpose.
Give one piece of leadership advice to new school leaders.	Be visible. Your whole school community needs to see you as part of the life and heartbeat of the school. By standing on the gates at drop off, joining students in the lunch hall, visiting lessons at different points during the day, taking a moment to speak to staff in the staffroom about their weekend, you begin to understand your school and the people within it. It also allows people to get to know you too, and on a day when things may be difficult, it reminds you of why we do what we do each day. You see the difference that you make to your school community.

Part 1 Key points

Navigating doubt

1. When awarded the privilege of the ultimate leadership position, recognise that this is only the beginning of learning to lead.
2. Take confidence from your closest allies to be your true self. Let their feedback refresh your humility so you can develop.

3. Be comfortable about working with less praise.
4. Find the communication style that fits with who you are as a leader – for me, that is speaking plainly.
5. Recognise the powerful impact of speaking from the heart and knowing when to show vulnerability as a leader.
6. Making poor decisions is a powerful reminder to think about how you make decisions – gather all the right information, challenge this, draw on your experience and check your bias.
7. Have the courage to U-turn when new information comes to light.
8. Spend some time in the cinema in your head to play out plausible scenarios and see potential outcomes from the eyes of others.
9. Forgetting is important but should not be at the expense of addressing tough challenges and creating positive change.
10. Make visibility a focus.
11. Recognise when you need to ask for help and avoid the *arrogance-veil trap*. Share the problem, use and build networks, and make sure you have a trusted mentor.

Part 2
EMBRACING CHALLENGE

Chapter 12

FACING SIGNIFICANT UNDERPERFORMANCE HEAD-ON

I have a very pleasant, large office at the front of the school, smartly decorated with a conference table for ten and a desk that is larger than my bathroom at home. Today, I can't sit at this desk or even look across my office. I seem compelled to look out of my window to plan what I need to say to a failing colleague – as if looking away, not actually looking at anything, will make what I am about to do a little easier. As I rock from one foot to the other, I shape my thoughts into the primary concerns, backed with a couple of examples. I routinely check the time and decide that it is time to face the issue head-on – serious underperformance. I call my colleague and ask them to come and see me, knowing the impact of that call and the effect of uncertainty that it will have inevitably caused. '*Why does he need to see me?*' I hear in the silence as I put the phone down and check the time again.

I now face the colleague at the conference table, crossing my legs and adopting a more casual position. I berate myself for this, out of a general kindness for others, as I know where I am going to lead this conversation. I know full well that I need to put the overall needs of the school first. I have the concerns ready to express. I need to face the issue.

'*I am concerned about your performance*', the words leave my mouth in slow motion and form a bullet that hits him in the shoulder. His body shudders and recoils. The next bullet hits the other shoulder with another concern and the example further opens the wound.

The knowledge that this is the right thing to do eases the grim reality of what I am doing. He is failing and I fire the final deadliest bullet. I have used these words before, and I know they wound. *'How did we get to this point where you have lost the trust of your team and where I have lost my trust in you?'*

Facing issues head-on, however difficult, career-changing and awkward, takes an absolute commitment to doing the right thing for the organisation. Difficult conversations must be based on carefully considered evidence and not a whim. We should place them within our own values of right and wrong. However much we fear or try to avoid the conversation, you just have to say it and express the concern. As I walk home, I remind myself that you have to act and get things done. It was the right thing to do. It is tempting to moan, to become negative, to make excuses, to judge and blame, but the only actual solution is to face tough conversations head-on.

Avoid moaning, negativity, making excuses, judgement and blame by facing tough conversations head-on.

REFLECTION QUESTION

What are the issues that you need to face head-on?

TASKS

1. Note the tough conversations that you have been avoiding.
2. Summarise for each of these the most fundamental reason for your concern and an example.
3. Begin the conversation.

Chapter 13
COVERING OFF IN A CRISIS

The world suddenly changed in April 2020; Covid-19 disrupted the equilibrium and the stability we took for granted in school.

We received news of a pending lockdown. Some pupils and staff started to self-isolate, but we kept open and dealt with letters asking us to close the school whilst the government said schools should stay open. Things developed at a pace, and we cancelled an exchange trip to Germany. Within a couple of weeks, we had to reduce the number of year groups in school due to staff absence. Then, the Prime Minister announced schools would close. This reduced our school population of over 2100 children and 300 staff onsite to 30 pupils per day. The rest of our school population was told to learn, teach and work from home.

You are constantly learning when you are a new school leader. It is interesting how your language as a leader develops and changes. We pick up phrases of those around us, creatively using new phrases and expressions. Surrounded by talented colleagues who ask questions and try to see solutions, combined with the magnitude of the crisis, created new phrases and new expressions. One of those new expressions, which we used repeatedly, was *'to cover off'* – not *'cover up'* or *'cover over'*, but *'cover off'*.

In a short period, we created a mini-school within our school for the children of key workers and vulnerable children. We shifted all working practices online. This included teaching and learning, line management, staff briefings and training. In the background, we studied the financial impact and also guidance on how pupils were to be given exam grades without sitting exams. We set up systems to support families with free school meals and created new safeguarding policies for new ways of working online.

We did this whilst staying positive, standing tall, but remembering to keep socially distanced. Being a new school leader in a period of rapid change creates new challenges and many *unintended consequences*. In my meetings with senior colleagues, they asked me question after question about scenarios I had never seen before – what do I do now? Working closely with them, I coped with this by facing into each question, trying to find a solution and then saying, *'does that cover off the issue?'*.

In other contexts, I said *'that will cover this off'*, *'how can we cover this off?'* or *'we can cover this off by ...'*. I have used this phrase hundreds of times and heard my team echoing the phrase back, *'I think if we respond in this way, it will cover off that concern'*.

This expression was useful, creating a practical and solution-faced approach. It showed strength to get things done when everyone was adapting to a moving equilibrium. People need clear direction, confidence and clarity when they are trying to cope with the upheaval of rapid social change. Language is important as a leader. We must let our own language adapt to the surrounding situation. This phrase allowed me to lead our response confidently in challenging times.

> *Language is important as a leader. Use phrases that set the direction with confidence.*

REFLECTION QUESTION

How do the phrases we use shape the language used by others we lead?

TASKS

1. Note the common phrases you use in the day-to-day of your leadership.
2. Do these phrases set a positive and action-focused narrative?
3. Do they set a negative narrative?

Chapter 14

ASSERTION

A colleague made a pointed comment, and I said we needed to take up the issue outside of the meeting. We didn't. The frustration didn't sit well. The next day, the same colleague asserted that *'all teachers think ...'*. *'We need to check the facts'*, I replied, frustrated. Later I asked for a comment about a document that we were working on, and the colleague replied without pause and asserted that *'all children do ...'* and then *'all children would ...'*. I'd had enough. I fired back *'stop'*. *'How do you know? You are making such broad generalisations?'*

Sharp words sometimes occur in the day-to-day exchanges of working in teams. I didn't like how other colleagues were being denied the space to think or space to talk. I didn't like the assertion. I didn't like this exchange.

The comments were being made quickly, with confidence and force. This kind of talk is dangerous if it goes unchecked within a team. It can send you down the wrong path, prejudicing thinking and even intimidating others. The claiming of airspace causes differing reactions. Some become angry and fight harder to claim back the space, others fade quietly into the background. I just made it worse by expressing my frustration. My sharp reaction could intimidate others. If the colleague who speaks first with such confidence is told to stop, then others might choose to be quiet to protect themselves. A communication issue had emerged and, if left unchecked, could negatively affect the team. It was time for an honest conversation, one-to-one.

My colleague knew straight away when I explained my concern, and they apologised. But how do you check against assertion? How do you know what is happening in your school? Who do you listen to? How do you know what you know? In our desire to lead change and do the right thing, it is important to act on the right information. Leaders set the direction, but they need pointing in the right direction.

There are different ways in which leaders can protect against the dangers of assertion. First, *seek the views of others*. I used to think that asking questions could lead to the truth and an excellent decision – most of the time this works. But those who are loud and those who speak first can influence a team. People need time to think and space to say what they think. When you need to know what all your team members think without the influence of the assertive one, I ask for colleagues to write their view first before we then share. This gives a much broader basis for an open and divergent exchange of ideas. Another strategy is to know your team so well that you bring in the *quiet-perceptive* type; give their ideas the status by directly asking them to say what they think.

Second, *seek discussion on valid sources of information*. Base decision-making on organised agendas with evidence-based reports. Ask about the sample size, check the data and ask for more information before making the final decision.

Third, I remind myself that leaders need to *check their own assertion*. Whilst I listen for assertions of others and try to check this against what I think I know, I remind myself that I might behave in the same way. I remind myself to keep an open mind. In short, whilst there may well be truth in an assertion, it is important to pause and seek understanding.

Sometimes as leaders, we face much quicker exchanges and it is these micro assertions that new leaders need to check. We don't always have the time to seek fully the views of others, seek discussion on evidence-based reports or remember to check our own assertions. One very simple strategy, though, is to pause and ask some simple questions. Why do you think that? Why do you say that? What is driving that comment? Trying to understand the assertions of others in everyday interactions acts as a break from going down blind alleyways. Challenging assertions can also open doors to new avenues of exploration and new ways of thinking.

> *Protect against the dangers of assertion by seeking fully the views of others, using valid sources of information and checking your own assertion.*

REFLECTION QUESTION

Are there colleagues in your team who have voices that dominate?

TASKS

1. Ask someone outside of your school to watch you lead a meeting. Ask them to analyse the contribution of others and how you react to assertion.
2. When you spot assertion, simply ask *'why do you think that?'*. Ask *'what is the real issue behind what you have said?'*.
3. What steps can you take to prevent assertion from impacting upon the effectiveness of your decision-making?

Chapter 15
KEEPING PERSPECTIVE

We need to keep perspective. My phone rang, and it was my wife. *'I've got some bad news'*, she said. I ask her what was wrong and I could hear her emotion between the words, *'we've lost the house'*. I tried to stay positive, gave words of reassurance and dashed through my work. I know, today, that I need to not be too late home. We had been trying to move house during the pandemic; we had lost one house, felt the pain of extending a lease on our apartment, found our new home, and then it fell through at the eleventh hour. Far worse things happen, but we were both cross and upset. New leaders need to remember that they, like their colleagues, have lives outside of school where things go wrong.

You hear many things as a leader, often the things that aren't going so well. You hear snippets of information, often an exaggerated version of events without the full context. These snippets tempt you to react and tease you into negativity.

You see many things as a leader, the good and the bad. It is all too easy to focus obsessively on the negative. You may have only glimpsed this for a moment, but it comes to dominate your thoughts. You focus on this, rather than the good that exists most of the time.

Negativity spirals and thoughts form a dark mood. You read an email with some criticism that doesn't seem to make sense but is yet so real in the eyes of the sender. You read a survey and see some data that concerns you and it is easy to fret. Doubt sets in.

This makes you cross with yourself and makes you question what you do.

In these moments, new leaders need to shift the human response of anger and upset to something much calmer. Trying to seek understanding first can keep you calm so you can then act on the facts. There is *usually* a reason for something happening and *always* a perspective you can take on how you see it.

We broke our bad news to our son, who was really looking forward to moving. He reminded me of how I should behave – a gentle nudge. He said, *'you'll sort it, it will work out in the end'*. It is important to keep perspective in the face of challenges. Think positively and have confidence in what you do.

Keep perspective and have confidence.

REFLECTION QUESTION

How can you keep perspective?

TASKS

1. List the multitude of reasons why you feel overwhelmed.
2. Identify the real issue behind why you have lost perspective and why you have stopped thinking logically.
3. Can you reframe this issue to form a calmer, more positive response?

Chapter 16
ECHO

Sometimes we simply fail to understand. This probably happens much more than we care to imagine. We create in our minds a false sense that we really understand our colleagues and that we know what people think. But sometimes we categorically and plainly misunderstand, misinterpret and miss the point.

I have met with many parents who have expressed concerns, and most of the time you gain an understanding and reach a resolution. On one occasion, the meeting took place very late in the day and the interaction was challenging and hostile from the very start. Tempers flared, the parents threw side concerns into the pot, interruptions were rife, and things were not going well. Far from being a smooth interaction before heading home, this was turning out to be a very bumpy and uncomfortable ride. And it was at this moment that, in the maelstrom of the exchange, I'd stopped understanding. As soon as the words left my mouth, *'maybe you have chosen the wrong school if you don't think the school is good enough'*, I realised I had failed. Defensive, projecting back my frustration, I'd stopped listening. It didn't need to end this way, and there was a much better way.

When we face the strongest attacks, even if they are only perceived, with triggers pressed and without red flags, we must try to take a step back and ask, *'what is the actual issue here?'*. People need to be understood. This is especially so when you are a leader. You don't have to act upon or agree with everything suggested, but you must make every effort to understand.

Closing your eyes for a moment may give the impression of concentrated listening. Writing notes when someone meets with you indicates that you take their views seriously. Nodding your head in agreement and saying *'Mmm'* gives reassurance and the impression that you understand. Simply giving time says you are listening and taking their views seriously. But this does not mean that you truly understand. You create a false sense of order that often veils the actual issue.

There are two sequential techniques that new leaders can use to avoid misunderstanding. First, ask a series of five questions, remembering to listen at the end of each:

1. what is the actual issue here?
2. but what is the actual issue here?
3. what are you not telling me?
4. and what else?
5. and what else?

Second, and this is the most important technique, use *echo back*. I stand back from all the words that I have just heard and try to cut through to the meaning, expressing back the words said to me with a succinct summary. I use language such as *'I am just going to pause there and explain what I am hearing. I want to check that I fully understand.'* Do this and then listen again and then offer a further *echo back*. Whilst this takes more time, it often saves you time in dealing with a follow-up complaint and further meetings.

Charles Horton Cooley (1902), an American sociologist, provides a very simple explanation of why this technique is so effective. For Cooley, we develop our sense of self by watching how others perceive us. He called this the *'looking glass self'*. We base our sense of self on the views of others through a mirror of social interaction. When we interact with others, we effectively create a mirror; judgements, perceptions, our sense of worth, and impressions move back and forth.

We imagine how we appear; we imagine the judgement of others of that appearance and react because of those perceived judgements. By using the echo technique, you are effectively saying *what you have to say matters*. I care enough to understand you properly and I take you seriously. This is a powerful impression to make, especially for new leaders.

The concept of the *'looking glass self'*, applied to leadership, asks us to *echo back* in a way to make others feel a positive sense of self-worth. *Echo back* works for me, across all meetings and all interactions.

> *Master how to make people feel understood. Seek to hear the real issue.*

REFLECTION QUESTION

How do you resolve a hostile complaint?

TASKS

1. When you next experience a challenging complaint, use the five sequential questions: what is the actual issue here? but what is the actual issue here? what are you not telling me? and what else? and what else?
2. Then echo back a simple summary to show you understand.
3. Seek resolution.

Chapter 17

BREATHING THROUGH YOUR FEET

I hadn't slept well because the radio interview, early the following morning, was on my mind. With my feet close together, trying to find a grounding, I sat at the side of my bed, rubbed my eyes before guiding myself through the darkness to the staircase, trying to not wake my family. I made some tea and attempted to wake my voice, humming, and saying a few sentences aloud. The phone rang and the researcher told me the name of the interviewer. He told me I would hear some music before my name would be introduced. He told me they were about to call Pat and asked me not to swear. This last piece of advice made me smile, as I wondered whether the BBC had listening devices in my home. Why would they say that to me? I wrote the name of the radio host at the top of my notebook and listened to the music – the latest emotional sentiments from Adele.

I thought about what Pat's morning would have been like and what she felt, listening to the music. Pat's son died by suicide in 2017. Dom was a kind-hearted young person, a talented artist and musician, who loved his friends and who wanted to live. When Dom died, Pat and her husband Jan asked me to lead the celebration of Dom's life, and my thoughts, listening to the music, took me to the moment where I walked to the front of the chapel, behind Pat, Jan and their son Greg. I gently touched Dom's coffin, and walked to the lectern, looked up and saw such sadness across the crowd of Dom's friends and loved ones. My thoughts took me to Pat and Jan, and then the interviewer spoke.

I had drifted but his voice snapped me back into the moment. My voice lodged itself in my throat, my sentences shortened, my speech became stilted and I couldn't see the sentences in my mind. The interviewer turned to Pat, and she spoke of her son and the need to raise awareness about suicide prevention. I then spoke about our Hope Walk for Dom, the number of children killed by suicide each year and the important charity, Papyrus.

When the interview finished, with a red face and a sigh, I phoned Pat and talked about how much admiration I have for her. We talked about how difficult it is to talk about suicide and agreed to never accept an early Saturday morning interview again, especially after the latest release of a heart-rending song about loss.

Despite preparing for the interview with the points I wanted to make, I hadn't prepared my mind and I let the emotion dent my thoughts. I needed to still my mind, allow the emotion to hit me, but then slow my speech by breathing properly. A talented drama teacher told me, *'pretend you are breathing through your feet'*. I needed to stand, with my legs grounded, apart, imagining the air coming in from my feet and out from my voice. I needed to still my mind so I could speak more clearly about Dom. I did this at the celebration of his life, so why had I struggled so much more today? Back then, I was very much thinking about Dom, whilst also being in control to support his family and our community. I focused on helping and communicating well. This experience on Saturday morning brought back what had happened, and I should have given more attention to my thoughts. The experience reminded me to prepare my mind and breathe through my feet.

We need to be forgiving of ourselves when we don't communicate how we would like or when we fall short at important points. But as new leaders, we owe it to others to be the best version of ourselves. This experience was a reminder to breathe through my feet and to calm my mind.

When faced with challenges, be kind to yourself.
Remember to breathe and calm your mind.

REFLECTION QUESTION

Why do leaders sometimes fail to communicate well?

TASKS

1. Think of an example where emotion or distraction has impacted your communication.
2. What steps could you take to prevent this?

Chapter 18

REAL COURAGE

I can't believe I didn't see it. I can't believe no one in my team saw it. There really was no excuse for not seeing it; we just weren't really looking.

A colleague didn't seem to be with us. His eyes were distant. And his previous joy in his role had faded. His ideas became more disconnected, and team meetings had agonising moments. That feeling when chairing a meeting, where the world slows down, and you glance in the eyes of others. His thoughts were unclear. Still, no one properly noticed.

I asked for his plan to be redelivered; thinking that being given a chance to repeat his work would surely put things right. He still lacked clarity and his proposal just wasn't what I wanted. I made a judgement. *'I'm just going to do it myself'*, *'we need to sort this out'*, I thought.

I think it is all too easy to see an issue through the judgemental lens of underperformance. We forget that people may have many things going on in their lives. Yes, it takes courage to face issues head-on because we must be brave to challenge what we think is not right. I am learning, however, that this is a simplistic view of courage. There is a much more meaningful role courage can play in leadership.

I sat with my colleague and faced the issue head-on. I expressed my concerns and, feeling courageous, we discussed whether the role was right for him. Looking back at this, I feel such shame that I felt courageous. I see this now as fake courage.

The individual in front of me looked back at me, broken and desperate. No words came out of him, his normally proud posture slumped, his hand placed to prop up his tired head. I saw it then. I said, '*I care about you, are you OK, what's wrong?*'

His emotion came out and said he didn't know why he felt the way he did. This was real courage. He talked about his family, how much his job meant, how he cared so much about the school and how he didn't feel himself. The bell went for the next lesson, but he wasn't ready to go out into the corridor under the gaze of others. I gave him some time alone. Hardly courageous, I stepped out of my office.

As the children walked past me, chatting with each other on their way to their next lesson, I was furious with myself. One of my closest friends had delivered the Mental Health First Aid course in school; all my senior team were trained. Many of my team had first-hand experience of supporting others with their mental health. I was cross, wrongly, with my suffering colleague – he had completed the training. Why had we all failed to see it?

I went back to my office, and we talked again. He needed some time, and he went for a walk outside. I encouraged him to talk with his wife, to talk to someone, anyone. He did just that and got the help he needed. Over time, I saw his confidence return. He came back, wiser and ready to lead again.

Courage in leadership is not always about hard and honest conversations. Courage is sometimes what you draw out of people when you remember your Green Cross Code. Courage is learning to stop, look and listen. Courage is letting others express they need help, getting help, recovering, encouraging, supporting and not writing people off. I am learning to be a better leader from the shameful error of not seeing what I plainly needed to see.

Have the courage to stop, look and listen. Have the courage to let others express that they need help, support them, and don't write people off.

REFLECTION QUESTION

What role does courage play in leadership?

TASKS

1. Stop, look and listen properly to your team.
2. Who are you looking at through the judgemental lens of underperformance?
3. What factors are at play that you are simply not seeing?

Chapter 19
INSPECTION

Schools in England operate within a high-stakes accountability system of school performance tables and Ofsted (Office for Standards in Education, Children's Services and Skills) inspection reports. In 1990, John Major was in power and, keen to put rigour into inspections, Ofsted hired many inspectors as Her Majesty's Inspectors (HMIs) and introduced a common inspection framework. By 1993, using this framework, all state-funded schools were subject to inspection. Ofsted published their reports for all to see. There were many *unintended consequences* of this inspection and regulatory structure, not least the *fear* in teachers and leaders of *'having Ofsted in'*.

In 2007, the school where I work achieved an outstanding grading and, in 2011, became exempt from further inspection unless significant concerns arose. By 2020, the conservative government lifted this exemption and outstanding schools, many not inspected for over a decade, became due for inspection.

Since the school's last inspection, the inspection framework – the standard by which we judge schools – has changed many times and the most recent framework sets a very high bar. Christopher Russell, National Director of Ofsted, said,

> *There's no doubt that under the current education inspection framework, outstanding is a challenging and exacting judgement to achieve. To achieve it, a school needs*

to fulfil all of the good criteria, securely and consistently. They then need to achieve additional outstanding criteria and they need to be performing exceptionally.
(Schools Week, 2021)

Because of the exacting nature of the new framework, since inspection resumed in September 2021, only 50 per cent of schools maintained their outstanding judgement. Under the extremely challenging new framework, Ofsted was keen to stress that a school may well be no longer judged as outstanding and be judged as good, even if the school improved since their last inspection (TES, 2022).

Like so many school leaders and teachers, the impending inspection was undoubtedly a source of fear and stress for me. New school leader, indeed! What do I do now? It was right to inspect the school after so long, but leading a school judged to be outstanding as a new headteacher created a fear of *'what if?'*. *'What if the outcome is "good", what if the outcome is "requires improvement", what if the outcome is "inadequate"?' 'What if I really mess this up and what if I lose my job?'* I tried to mask the fear of *'what if?'*, but the weight of doubt can be hard to hide. Leaders and teachers up and down the country face the relentless worry about *'what if?'*.

'What's up?' my wife asked. *'You seem to have a lot on your mind.'* I explained my worries, and she reassured me that I was doing the right things to prepare. I remember going for a long walk with her. After an hour, the everyday chat of practical domesticity often runs dry – things that needed doing to our house, who was going to give the cats their flea treatment, etc. Our talk then shifted to the much more meaningful talk of dreams and aspirations. My aspiration for the school was to remain outstanding, but before too long, my thoughts had returned to fear and doubt.

I look back now and think about my plans for if it all went wrong. There would be no way I could stay in the town where I live. I would need to run away after my dismissal. We would sell everything we owned, ask my sister-in-law to take the cats and move to Poland.

My wife spoke the language, and we had had many happy times in Krakow. We would rent an apartment and start our lives again. I would find any job I could and learn the language. My wife seemed to be OK with the plan, or humoured me, knowing that it gave me solace. This ridiculous thought process and the fear of *'what if?'* was the backing track of being a new leader – an unpleasant piece of music that occasionally faded before turning itself back up. It had a life of its own.

We were away at the weekend, celebrating the sixtieth birthday of a close friend in Northumbria. Driving back home to Harrogate, thoughts drifting, I said to my wife, *'I bet it's this week'*. *'What's this week?'* she asked. *'I think I will get the call for an inspection.'* On Tuesday 8 March 2022, Ofsted informed me they would inspect the school the following day.

The phone rang at exactly 10am. I don't know if I knew it was them, but I somehow felt I knew. Who calls at exactly 10am? Picking up the phone, I heard our receptionist sounding very serious. *'I have a lady on the phone from Ofsted.'* Turning my notebook to a blank page, I took the call.

The person from Ofsted must be used to headteachers who appear to have the inability to note the simplest things. I asked her to repeat the name of the lead inspector so I could write it down. Despite her clear voice, I still couldn't process the name. I think it was the initial panic. Looking back at my notes now, I see a child-like scrawl.

She informed me I would receive another call in an hour's time. This would last for around 90 minutes with the lead inspector.

I put the phone down and called Kirstie, my Associate Head, and Tim, the Deputy Head. Our plan needed to be put into action.

An hour later, we sat huddled around my desk with the phone on a long extension cable. Having all come to terms with the news that inspectors would be in school tomorrow and after encouraging words of *'we can handle this'*, *'no more waiting'*, *'we're ready'*, the phone rang again.

Sometimes fear and doubt make you think something is going to be far harder or worse than it is. The lead inspector seemed experienced and put us at ease. I knew we needed to be clear and confident. Relationships and trust matter, so when he reminded me we hadn't had a full inspection since 2007, I said, *'I know, we've been waiting for your call'*. Why I felt it necessary to evoke the language of a Bond villain, I do not know, but we nervously took our first laugh together. Kirstie later followed this with a much more sophisticated observation about the irony of the all-male inspection team on International Women's Day.

The call lasted 109 minutes and 28 seconds. We felt positive and felt that we had set out our stall well for the next two days.

With our Year 8 parent consultation evening until 8pm, we had very little time to brief the staff, so we spoke with them at lunchtime and in a small window of time at the end of the school day before staff went online to talk with parents. We had delivered a detailed briefing for staff at the start of the year, so I felt relieved that none of the information I was sharing with them now was new. This allowed us to relax into our briefing, use some humour and focus on building confidence – the mantra was *'we are ready, we can handle this'*. I could see a range of different thoughts and feelings in the room – worry, focus, hunger to get it done and togetherness for what we were about to face. Later in the afternoon, we briefed all the children through an online assembly and wrote to parents to inform them of what was happening.

We worked late into the evening, printing class seating plans for the inspectors with key information about each child. My senior team kept checking in with me to tell me they had completed their part of the plan. Our teachers finished the parent consultation evening late and then turned their focus to making sure their lessons were ready. Eleven hours in; only 45 hours until we would know the result. I needed to control my fear and keep cool. I repeated in my mind, *'positive, confident and clear'*. I needed to calm my thoughts and breathe through my feet. I was grateful for how the whole staff rallied together.

Day one

I looked at my watch, 7.55am, and then glanced out of my office window to the car parking bays. At five-second intervals between each of the seven cars, they arrived in a convoy.

Kirstie, Tim and I greeted them at reception and walked them through the school to the room that was set up for them to use as their base. As we engaged in conversations about journey times, where they worked, and how the contractors built the new pupil entrance during the lockdown, I felt like a footballer walking out onto the pitch with the opposition, then like a barrister walking into a court, then like a boxer.

From that moment forth, the day flew by with meetings with leaders in maths, English, modern foreign languages, PE, art and history before many lesson visits across the school. They asked question after question, interviewed groups of pupils from the lessons they visited, and then met with groups of staff. I spent a large part of the day with the lead inspector in lesson visits and between this checked in with senior colleagues and my CEO, who monitored feedback coming back from staff. Then, the fire alarm went off.

We ran out of the office to silence the alarm before confirming whether we needed to evacuate the entire school. A fast-paced game of dodgeball had taken place and the ball had hit the sensor. The PE teacher smiled nervously, sighed and dropped his head – an apology that needed no words. After a private moment of colourful language, I informed the lead inspector about what had happened.

The inspectors summarised what they had seen during the first day and, whilst positive, some of their comments concerned me. Without a doubt, we had to step things up and show how we were implementing the curriculum consistently in lessons. Working with the lead inspector, we prepared the next day with an agreement to visit science, drama, English, modern foreign language and geography. Staff had worked with total focus and control throughout the day. We knew that tomorrow was going to be even more rigorous. They were revisiting areas to check their initial judgements.

During the first day, they had been collecting evidence around behaviour and attitudes, leadership, special educational needs provision, the sixth form and the overall personal development of our children. Senior leaders would tomorrow meet with inspectors about each of these areas, explaining our work and answering questions. Meetings would also take place with separate groups of boys and girls in the lower school and sixth form pupils; there would be meetings about safeguarding, about reading and a meeting with our governors.

Kirstie, Tim and I left school late. It felt like we were drawing at half-time. I was worried about Tim. He had slept very little and hadn't eaten since the phone call. Only 21 hours until we knew the result.

Day two

I woke with the feeling you have during exams – you are free for only a moment, then you remember you have an important test to get through. By the end of today, whatever the result, it would be over. I walked to school in the gap between night and day, listening to music and thinking about the important messages that I needed to communicate to staff. I needed to project calm and confidence, whilst ensuring that staff responded to the feedback gleaned on the first day. Before I spoke, I carefully scripted what I wanted to say and checked with Kirstie. In high-stake situations, I find it much easier to communicate. The magnitude of the event can evaporate any doubt you have about yourself. You become so invested in trying to serve your community that you wrap yourself only in the moment. We were ready to push on once more – staff rallied again.

Then the lead inspector knocked the wind out of me. Overnight, he had looked at the responses from the pupil and parent survey. Whilst overall the responses were positive, there were a couple of responses that didn't fit with what they saw in the school the previous day. The responses surprised me. Kirstie and I scrambled to explain why this might have occurred. The lead inspector listened intently but explained that they were going to check this during the day.

Throughout the second day, the questions intensified, and we then faced criticism around the speed at which it took to generate some further evidence about attendance. They then asked us for even more information about attendance at different sub-group levels. The data was hard to extract from our newly installed managed information system. Children were being pulled out of lessons to be asked additional questions. My senior team were tiring, and it felt like we were really being tested. I sent a text to my wife, *'things are not going well, I'm not sure where this will fall'*. In corridors, we smiled and willed each other forward.

It was time to find out the result. Tim, Kirstie and I, supported by our CEO and one of our governors, stood outside their base, ready to go in. The room was set out for the inspectors to sit with the lead inspector at the head of the table. We were sitting in a line, on a row of desks behind theirs. We were onlookers to the judgement that they were about to make.

How we prepared

The new inspection framework inspectors used to evaluate our school was introduced in 2019. This was the year I became a headteacher. I needed to be practical about my worries at the time and focus my energy on preparing the school. Like many headteachers, despite the challenges of the new framework, Kirstie and I were excited about the focus on the quality of the curriculum. Our first step was to find someone who had trained as an inspector under the new framework to help our faculty leaders. This started the process of iteration and practice, where all areas reviewed their subject curriculum across each key stage, across the school. A mammoth task of research and review, sequencing and re-sequencing the schemes of learning to ensure that pupils could learn more, remember more and do more.

We then worked with an exceptional individual who had many years of experience as an inspector and who carried out reviews in each area. We started this work just before the pandemic. It would have been easy to stall this work with all we faced during that time, but we kept the momentum going. Online and when back in school, this involved faculty leaders practising talking about the intent of their curriculum with confidence and showing how we went beyond the national curriculum.

We then visited lessons to check that what they were saying was taking place in the classroom; we were looking for a seamless thread. I knew we needed to drive our preparation forward, but it was challenging, with all the pressures on schools during the pandemic, such as summer school, generating exam grades and trying to keep the school open and functioning.

In September 2021, other headteachers were talking about schools that had received visits from Ofsted. These schools, like us, hadn't faced inspection for a long time, so I knew our inspection was closing in on us. I needed to tune us in. I invited a colleague to recreate the meetings we were likely to face.

Kirstie and I carried out an exchange with a school in a similar position as us; we gave their staff the opportunity to talk about their curriculum and their headteacher and deputy repeated the process in our school. We then carried out a further two-day review in school with a trained inspector and local headteacher. After each experience, we were meticulous and relentless about addressing any feedback they had and coached staff on how to perform with confidence.

We trained our governors and prepared a document that answered the questions they were likely to face. We asked a previous inspector to check our entire website to ensure that all the information needed was in place. The first term of that year was difficult for my senior leadership team. I tried to hide my fears and worries about inspection, but they undoubtedly spilled over. I remember Kirstie talking to me about her worries over the pressure I was putting on colleagues. Leading through a high-stakes accountability system is a balancing act. You are trying to drive things forward and get things done, whilst trying not to create toxic stress. I felt this myself, so I know I didn't always get this right for me or for my colleagues.

The outcome

Listening to the inspectors go through each bullet point of the framework, assiduously ticking off where they had seen what they had needed to see, I hoped that all the work in preparation would pay off. I listened to their comments about our school and thought about how much of what they see are routines, practices and traditions that layer up, year after year. This judgement would be about much more than the actions of any one leader, it would be about the culture and the overall quality of education at our school, achieved by the collective action of the whole.

After two days of rigorous inspection, with a team of seven inspectors, Ofsted reached the judgement that the overall effectiveness of our school was *'outstanding'*. They judged the school to be outstanding in all five areas of the framework: the quality of education, behaviour and attitudes, personal development, leadership and management and sixth-form provision. As the inspectors shook our hands, my plan about Poland vanished. I simply felt pride in my colleagues and in the culture of our school. The intensity of the final meeting will stay with me, the memory of Kirstie trying frantically to take notes, the pent-up emotion and the gradual relief as the judgement became clear.

The inspectors returned to their base and packed up before we walked them back through the school to the main reception. Kirstie and I were holding bunches of daffodils. Our governor had bought them for us – an act of kindness because, whatever the outcome, they were a sign of new beginnings. A new chapter had indeed started, and we talked about some things we needed to follow up on, but mainly how we needed to catch up on lots of emails. We needed to go home to our families.

As I walked through the front door of my home, I remembered that the last text I sent my wife was at 10am, explaining that things weren't going well. She knew, though, when she saw me that things were OK, and I could see her relief. The worries we hold, and the pressure we handle, transcend the place where we work to our closest loved ones. I need to manage this better in the future and remember that leadership should never be about a self-absorbed *'me'*. I apologised.

The inspection team carefully briefed us that the report needed to be checked and would go through a period of review before we could officially share the result. I asked the lead inspector about how headteachers communicate the outcome with their teams before the result is official. He smiled and said, *'I'll leave that with you'*. Kirstie and I talked about how we were going to inform staff after the inspectors left. We decided we would brief the senior leadership team in the morning and then meet the entire staff in our lecture theatre.

The senior team walked into my office, looking sullen and concerned. Within minutes, their relief was palpable – some cried, some giggled and some just sat back, sighing and smiling. I explained that the outstanding outcome wasn't official, so we could only really say that *'the inspection couldn't have gone better'*. They had all been carrying their own fears and worries about inspection.

Kirstie and I walked into the lecture theatre with the entire staff seated, searching for the outcome in our facial expressions and body language. Just as I would start an assembly, I stepped to the front and paused. I extended the pause, slightly longer than I needed, and with a smile and an upward glance, I could express the outcome without words.

I remember feeling such a powerful sense of solidarity and togetherness throughout what seemed to be endless applause. My eyes scanned the room, and I could see staff reacting in different ways – whooping, some crying, smiling and lots of clapping. I looked at Kirstie and felt proud of all the work staff had put in to reach this point. I can't remember the words used to express my gratitude, appreciation and thanks to the staff. I have instead a photographic picture in my mind of that briefing – a flashbulb memory, the closing of one chapter before the next. I then remember thinking, *'Kirstie is next to me, but I can't see Tim?'*

You see people for who they really are when working under such pressure. Tim copes with incredible pressure and simply gets the job done. I rarely witness Tim moaning and when he does, he isn't really moaning. We were walking the Yorkshire Three Peaks, and the day was drawing in as we approached the summit of Pen-y-Ghent. With tired legs and the sense of urgency to finish the walk before dusk, I asked Tim if he was OK. '*I don't like this me*', he said, laughing. '*I like the old me, the me before this walk, any me, not this me.*'

I remember visiting the Outwood Bound centre on the shores of Ullswater in the Lake District with him. We were undertaking an experience weekend for teachers, investigating whether to introduce more outdoor education into our school curriculum. One activity involved jumping into the lake – a ritual devised during the Second World War to help young sailors learn survival skills and gain experience of submersion in harsh conditions. We walked along the jetty to jump in. Tim looked up questioningly, gently shook his head and smiled. Then this gentle giant jumped into the lake.

There are colleagues like Kirstie and Tim that if you had to be stuck in a cave with anyone, you would want it to be them. They would do anything to help – they have a steely determination to sort things out. When I told them we had received the call from the inspectors, I saw the same expression as when Tim jumped in the lake and when he approached the summit of Pen-y-Ghent. I saw in Kirstie's eyes what I see every day, acknowledgement of another puzzle or challenge that just needed to be cracked. During the inspection, they went through meeting after meeting, calmly talking through our work and providing evidence. They worried about what they said and worried about what they didn't say. Like any exceptional colleagues, they really cared.

I still don't know where Tim was when we told the staff the outcome, but there is, however, a lesson to leaders for colleagues like this. We lean on them because we trust they will lead us out of the cave. In doing so, we push the hardworking to work harder, undoubtedly, making personal sacrifices. Others also miss the opportunity to learn how to lead us out of the cave. We need to look after professionals like Kirstie and Tim, whilst also developing the next generation.

Since the inspection, I see in Tim and Kirstie a new confidence. I feel the same confidence, but it isn't what I thought it would feel like. It is a calmer confidence as I continue to strive to develop as a leader; to think now about how to lead into our immediate future.

Leading through such high-stakes inspection sharpens your thinking to reflect on the next inspection and how you build, train and develop the team to not only further improve the school but be even better prepared for the next challenge. I still experience that feeling of being an imposter, especially when I rest from leading during the holidays, *'can I do it?'*, *'am I the right person for this privileged role?'*, but as my time in this role grows, that voice of doubt softens. This experience gave me confidence in how I work under pressure, helped me to develop as a leader and made me think about how I and others can develop next.

> *Vulnerability is OK. Have and lean on the good people around you.*

REFLECTION QUESTION

Given the high-stakes nature of inspection, what would be the most effective, helpful and positive way to regulate schools?

Chapter 20
WORK AND REST

I worked every evening and weekend in my bedroom during my schooling. My father would say to me *'don't overdo it, all work and no play, make Neil a dull boy'*. I enjoyed working in the evening and on weekends. It consumed me, and I wanted to do well. His words have stuck with me, especially whilst starting out as a new leader, and during the challenges of leading in a pandemic.

From mid-March to the end of May 2020, the Department of Education issued 148 new guidance documents and updates to schools. These documents typically arrived late in the evening, often at a weekend and days after snippets of information were released in government press releases. The guidance was rarely clear and sometimes contained errors. The Institute for Government rightly described the guidance that schools received from December 2020 to January 2021 as a *'blizzard'*. *'All work and no play'* rang true in the last few months of 2020 with endless guidance, contact tracing every weekend for confirmed positive Covid-19 cases in school, and the pressures of staff and pupils falling ill. Just before the Christmas break of 2020, attendance in school was 50 per cent. Work was hard.

I remember breaking up for the holiday, tired and snapping at others. Neil was more than a *'dull boy'*, he was a grumpy and less effective leader. I felt I had no choice with all that was going on. I just didn't rest. The volume of work was too much for me to plan anything outside of school. I wasn't complaining or trying to be a hero leader, it was just what the situation demanded.

I knew that, day by day, I was becoming less effective and less productive. I took solace in thinking about rest and what I hoped to do when work lifted. But I knew it was time to stop – I dreamed of doing something different, enjoying the warmth of the sun and time away. My mind was forcing me to do something different. I look back at the time and think how important it is that new leaders approach rest with as much intention as we approach work.

The habits of high-performing individuals fascinate me – not just how they behave at work but how they approach rest. How do they create separation from work, how do they control their time and how do they engage in totally different pursuits, even if using the same skills, from work? Charles Darwin seemed to approach work with as much intention as he did rest. He famously worked for an hour and a half, then responded to letters, then completed another hour and a half of work. At noon he went for a long walk, then had lunch, then had a nap, then went for a further walk before another hour of work.

New leaders should embrace rest with intention – treat rest seriously and make sure they put genuine effort into this area. I spend time with my family, nap, play the piano, walk, exercise and go to the cinema – all with the purpose of resting. I take breaks. And I seem to achieve so much more after rest.

> *Leaders must embrace rest with intentionality if they want to increase their productivity.*

REFLECTION QUESTION

How can you approach rest with intentionality?

TASKS

1. List the bad behaviours that occur when you are tired and working without rest.
2. Why is it crucial to approach rest with intentionality?
3. Structure rest into your daily routine.

Part 2
SUMMARY

Challenge, like doubt, seems like an inevitable experience when taking on a new leadership role. One of the most common challenges is tackling underperformance, which is best dealt with by facing the tough conversation head-on. Using positive phrases, and setting the direction with confidence, can help you to navigate difficulty, but be careful not to let others take you down the wrong path when they proffer strong opinions. Remember to seek fully the views of others, use valid sources of information and check your own beliefs.

It is easy to catastrophise as a new leader. The act of trying to keep perspective and simply having confidence that you will sort the situation out can lead you calmly out of a blind alley of perceived disaster. Stepping up into leadership opens you to challenge and sometimes hostility. Master, therefore, how to make people feel understood by trying to hear the real issue at hand. Then, remember, that leaders get it wrong and underperform. Be kind to yourself, remember to breathe and calm your mind.

Leadership is often fast-paced so it is important, at times, to put the brakes on to stop, look and listen. It takes courage to slow down and let others express their need for help and support. Don't just write people off. Inevitably, you will face some difficult circumstances as a new leader. Build around you a team of colleagues who you know inside-out and who you would trust in times of difficulty. Remember that it is OK to be vulnerable as a leader. Make sure you have and lean on the good people around you. Finally, and very simply, make sure you get enough rest.

Part of navigating challenges is also about having the right mindset, which we will explore in Part 4 on mindsets and culture. Matthew Partington, headteacher at Roundhay School, makes this link between embracing challenge and the importance of culture in the table below. After that, we will focus, in Part 3, on the basics of leading every day.

Part 2 Case study

Matthew Partington on embracing challenge

Name	Matthew Partington
Setting	Roundhay School, Leeds – all through school of 2467 pupils
Role	Headteacher
If you could give two pieces of advice to a new school leader to help them embrace challenge, what would you say?	Ensure that your entire mindset is shaped by your values. Let *'ethical leadership'* be your absolute non-negotiable and so much more than lip service. Serving the interests of your pupils, staff and community is way more important than *'ticking boxes'* to chase accountability measures or obsessing about Ofsted.
	The most effective leadership of challenge and culture happens when you are with people. Aim to spend as little time at your desk as possible: prioritise spending time on the corridors, in classrooms or on the school grounds. A positive and purposeful school culture cannot be built and maintained by leaders who constantly sit at a computer.

What is the most important leadership book to you?	Sinek, S (2014) *Leaders Eat Last: Why Some Teams Pull Together and Others Don't.* London: Penguin.
Why is this book important?	It details the fundamental importance of leaders and organisations being guided by a strong moral purpose, not only in decision-making, but also how they support and care for the people they lead. The book presents a powerful argument that the greatest and most effective leaders leave their ego at the door; personal accountability, integrity and trust are essential ingredients in building a loyal and committed team of staff. The central message of this book is crucial: stick to your values and put the growth and interests of others first. Then comes the bountiful reward of a truly cohesive, highly impactful organisation with real hunger for continued success.
Give one piece of leadership advice to new school leaders.	It's not about you. Ensure that staff are given full credit for their achievements, because you certainly couldn't have done it without them.

Part 2 Key points

Embracing challenge

1. Avoid moaning, negativity, making excuses, judgement and blame by facing tough conversations head-on.
2. Language is important as a leader. Use phrases that set the direction with confidence.
3. Protect against the dangers of assertion by seeking fully the views of others, using valid sources of information and checking your own assertion.
4. Keep perspective and have confidence.
5. Master how to make people feel understood. Seek to hear the real issue.
6. When faced with challenges be kind to yourself. Remember to breathe and calm your mind.
7. Have the courage to stop, look and listen. Have the courage to let others express they need help, support them and don't write people off.
8. Vulnerability is OK. Have and lean on the good people around you.
9. Leaders must embrace rest with intentionality if they want to increase their productivity.

Part 3
LEADING EVERY DAY: THE BASICS

Chapter 21
CURIOSITY

I listened to the Prime Minister with the inevitable announcement of another lockdown and the closure of the school, again. I didn't realise then that the following six weeks would teach me a powerful lesson in the relationship between curiosity and leadership. I haven't thought about curiosity before, other than as a polite form of being nosy.

School closed again and as we went back online we followed our school timetable, delivering live lessons to maintain the normal routines for our pupils. Normally, as leaders in schools, we walk the corridors, look in classrooms and talk with children and teachers. We check what is happening in our school. I have never thought about this, however, in terms of *'being curious'* – maybe because the information I sought was so easy to find within a short walk from my office. At the thought of all that learning online, with thousands of exchanges taking place, I became curious. How were children learning online?

I stared at the invitation link in my email to join a lesson and decided that it was time to press the link. Slightly nervous, I enjoyed the moment of reprieve when the computer told me to sit in the lobby. I made sure that my camera and mic were off. I thought about how polite this must seem to the teacher who was giving me permission to enter, rather than just having me striding into the room.

Being back in the classroom, albeit virtually, was a great feeling. The exchange of ideas, the modelling by the teachers, the gentle use of humour to build trust, the praise, and the framing and shaping of learning in the hands of an expert professional inspire you. My curiosity satisfied, I understood why many positive messages were coming into school.

Curiosity, however, appears to be more complicated than that. I felt more curious and wanted more, much more. Over the following weeks, I joined music lessons, science lessons, maths lessons, English lessons and business lessons. Each lesson allowed me to answer more and more questions I had about online learning; how do you engage pupils, how do you structure learning, how do you pitch the lesson, how do you model learning, how do you start and how do you end a lesson online and how do you give effective feedback?

My time in class achieved much more than answers to some of these questions. Each teacher had kindly invited me to join – they were humble and open to a virtual visit. I felt that by thanking them and praising them for all the great practice, I could transform my initial curiosity into something more. I could share the learning with other colleagues. In doing this publicly in whole staff briefings, I could praise them but also share the excellent techniques I saw.

I found that curiosity not only allowed me to engage with the teachers of the lessons I joined but also with our wider teaching staff. I shared my enthusiasm for what I was seeing and my appreciation for delivering a full timetable, day in and day out, online. Curiosity helped me to develop a fuller understanding of what teachers were experiencing. This gave greater depth to my understanding and helped me to make better decisions. Exercising my curiosity gave me the knowledge to show genuine appreciation.

Durkheim, one of the founding fathers of sociology, talked about how beliefs and values create a *collective conscience* (Giddens, 1972). New leaders can shape the *collective conscience*, and this can come from the curiosity expressed by the leader. What I learnt in this lockdown is that curiosity, and a genuine interest in learning in the classroom, fostered the sharing of great practice and a positive narrative about delivering a whole curriculum, with high-quality teaching, online. A *collective conscience* based on a common purpose to deliver great teaching. By fostering curiosity, you gain insight from which you build understanding. This can then be used to help you to communicate with colleagues and galvanise action. New leaders would be wise to respond to the question *'what now?'* with *'get curious'* about what people do.

Unleash curiosity, helping you to gain insight from which you build understanding. Do this positively and with praise to create a purposeful collective conscience.

REFLECTION **QUESTION**

What is the link between curiosity and effective leadership?

TASKS

1. At the start of a new school term, write five questions about your school that you are curious to understand.
2. Go out and look. Talk to your pupils and colleagues.
3. How can you use this information to galvanise action?

Chapter 22

PROCESS, NOT PLACE

For the past seven years, every second weekend in January, our senior leadership team left school early on Friday afternoon and headed away for a planning weekend. I packed my travel bag on Thursday evening and rushed to complete all my work on Friday before trying to shift into planning mode in a nice Yorkshire hotel. With a quick change of clothes on arrival and the yearly snow on Saturday morning, this became a new year routine. We adopted the mantra of *'sometimes you have to step outside of school, to work on school'* and this, combined with the innovative outputs from the weekend over many years, justified the planning weekend. The weekend stopped because of the pandemic. We had to adapt, and I learnt that sometimes process is more important than the place.

School had been closed, except for children of key workers and vulnerable children, and learning had gone fully online with live lessons. Exams were cancelled and the government had set the expectation that all children needed to be mass tested for Covid-19 before they could return. Whilst certainly not normal, the routine of the school day and rhythm of our usual meetings maintained a semblance of normality.

I walked home in the dark of winter, accompanied by the sound of car wheels driving over melting snow, and with the weight of my rucksack and the weight of children not in school, I remembered the previously forgotten routine of our planning weekend. The pandemic might take away the weekend, but it didn't need to take our collective efforts to plan innovation and positive change in our school. The following morning, we discussed this in our morning meeting and the senior team members were keen to set aside some afternoons for planning in a large, socially distanced space, with no distractions, just the team, research, ideas, challenge and teamwork.

The process was simple. Our development plan focuses on three pillars – culture, curriculum, and teaching and learning. All are underpinned by our school's core purpose of excellence for every child. This provided the backdrop to our planning. New members of the team talked freely about their first term in school. New colleagues breathe new life into our school, so it is important to hear their honest reflections and the areas they wish to focus on. Seasoned colleagues presented research and evidence to spark ideas for change. And we gave time between sessions to pause, think, laugh, challenge and express different views. We pulled things together at the end with some independent work: what three initiatives would you identify as our priority, what haven't you said that you feel you should, and if you were to identify one area of focus with the most potential impact, what would that be? Finally, we left our ideas to rest.

The planning time gave me the opportunity to simply observe. Erving Goffman (1959) said that a bicycle offers the most effective research tool for sociologists. You ride to the heart of the action, park up and watch. I thought of this and imagined my bike parked in the corner. I observed different behaviours, not fixed, but shifting throughout our time together.

The *quiet-perceptive*. These individuals think deeply, never dominate in meetings, and, given the space, have a lot to say. You may not always like what is being said, as it can often challenge you, but this type needs to be heard. I have a couple of these types in my team, and they are change-makers.

Second, the *joined-up*. These individuals plan and plan again. They carry out all the research and layer new initiatives on top of old ones. These types present with confidence and benefit from challenge. This allows you to see how they cope when something throws their plans off-course. Is the evidence that they base their ideas upon valid? I encourage others to question what these types have to say.

Third, the *questioner-challenger*. This type poses questions that force you to think. Their questions help move the discussion forward by sparking alternative points of view or different courses of action. Be careful, though, as you must remember to encourage them to say what they think, especially if their questions are ignored.

Fourth, the *brave*. These individuals say what they think, express alternative ideas and don't care if we challenge the idea back. They spark thought and help also to move things along.

Finally, the *improver-learner*. Sometimes people reveal themselves in such an intense setting and come across as less prepared and not as coherent in their thoughts. For them, with feedback and support, this will be the beginning of a journey to better performance in this kind of setting. They need to know that their performance fell short and that they need to prepare and contribute more effectively.

All the types, and all the differences, make the planning effective. We should show compassion for all because expressing ideas, delivering presentations, and challenging each other needs careful balance as if you were on a tightrope. Observing the different roles and shifting between them tells me the team is functioning well. Ideas and challenges dominate, not a single behaviour type. Trust in one another allows this to happen.

Over the coming weeks, we revisited the ideas at our normal senior leadership team meeting; we carried out further research, and we put ideas to different groups so that it prepared us for communicating our plans to the entire staff. Through a process of gradual refinement, we developed our plan.

I listened to my team explain the new proposals, the product of iteration and team refinement. I realised that the process of planning and ideation is much more about working together than where the planning takes place.

Create a time for your team to work collectively, without distraction, on future directions.

REFLECTION QUESTION

What is the most effective change or innovation that you have implemented in school?

TASKS

1. Work out the process, not the place, you want to use to carry out your planning meeting.
2. Identify the behaviour types in your team when you are planning together. Are you hearing the voices and drawing on the strengths of all your team?
3. Let the agreed outcome rest before you then refine.

Chapter 23

SMILING

In 1934, George Herbert Mead's pupils published a book called *Mind, Self and Society* that would change how we think about everyday social interaction (Mead, 1934). Teaching at the University of Chicago, Mead didn't publish books but lectured about the formation of the self and how we learn to interact with others based on the creation of shared meaning. Human gestures take on meaning through human interaction. As children, we learn the symbols of society and the gestures of everyday life. We learn the meaning of gestures in play: frowns, smiles, eye contact, looking away, surprise and sad faces. In playgrounds across the country, we learn the rules of everyday interaction. Mead's ideas are all too real as pupils interact with each other again after various lockdowns.

Schools are places of social interaction. When schools reopened, our pupils reminded us of the importance of human interaction, the importance of saying hello, and the importance of gestures that we experience when we spend time with others. I stood outside the school to greet pupils before they took their Covid-19 test to return to school. We hadn't seen the pupils since December. We exchanged simple words. *'Hello, good to see you, how are you?'* *'Good, good to see you, Sir, how are you?'* It wasn't the words alone that made the meaning. It was the positivity of our interaction, being present to smile and connecting again. This real human interaction is what I missed during lockdown.

Many young people were nervous about returning to school in the face of tests, masks and social distancing. Yet, there is something very simple that we can always do to help smooth the way for pupils. It goes beyond Covid-19 and speaks to the heart of what it means to be human.

One of our teachers deploys this most advanced and powerful teaching technique to the highest standard, *the smile*. He greets all children, all parents and all staff with the warmest and kindest of smiles. A smile that sings of confidence, care and connection. When I think of this teacher, I smile, and when pupils interact with him, they smile. Research tells us time and time again of the benefits of smiling for reducing stress and blood pressure, boosting the immune system and elevating our mood. It makes sense to smile like him, unleashing the contagion of positive connection.

It is easy to forget to smile at work. As the term passes and colleagues tire, heads can drop. We wrap ourselves up in a world of tasks that need to be done. We can forget about others as we hurry along the corridor to sort something out. Challenging agenda items and difficult meetings turn our smiles upside down as we concentrate on finding solutions. The strenuous reality of what some children and colleagues face in their daily lives can take away the joy that we can find from working with others.

When we welcomed pupils back to school after lockdown, we remembered to smile and say, '*Hello, great to see you, how are you?*' We showed empathy for the challenges that they faced and showed our gratitude for how they coped. We had spent far too much time in online meetings that were not always as productive as we would like and that didn't allow us to connect properly. We shouldn't need lockdowns to make us appreciate the need for smiling with others. New leaders would be wise to simply remember, whatever the challenge and point in the term – smile.

Smiling signifies confidence, care and connection. Remember to do it from the very beginning in your new role and every day.

REFLECTION **QUESTION**

What are the gestures that leaders can make to positively impact others?

TASKS

1. Your diary is full, you have many emails to reply to, calls to make. You have an endless list of tasks. Your smile has turned upside down. Think about how you are now presenting to others.
2. Pause.
3. Reset and re-engage in positive meaningful interaction.

Chapter 24
SAYING THANK YOU

One of our site staff struck me as a man of politeness. He had successfully run his own business before retiring a few years ago. When I interviewed him, he explained how bored he was and how he needed to work. He must be 20 years older than me, much wiser and more worldly, but he always refers to me as '*Sir*'. He always says '*thank you*'. He left retirement to work as one of our site staff.

One of the cleaners, who everyone knows for her larger-than-life charm, works in the same way. Every day, when she can, she generously brings me a coffee, and when I extend kindness in return, she says '*thank you*'. She says this with warmth, appreciation and sincerity.

Both of them remind me of the importance of being polite and saying, '*thank you*'. When you are new to a role, it is easy to be misguided in thinking all your new leadership initiatives, so impressive in their invention, will win hearts and minds. There is, however, a much simpler alternative to building relationships and rapport. Be polite and say '*thank you*' well.

Saying thank you is important as a leader. Most people want to feel that they are useful, and they also want to feel valued. Saying '*thank you*' helps you to achieve this. Looking a colleague in the eye, slowing down and sincerely saying '*thank you*' is crucial. You are taking notice, making colleagues visible and saying, '*you have helped, and I appreciate you*'.

When both my colleagues thank me, they don't simply say *'thank you'*, they also add what they are thanking me for. This makes their appreciation meaningful and clearly understood. New leaders would be wise to learn from this: *'Thank you for your detailed report. You gave me all the information that I need and it was really clear.'*

Saying thank you in front of larger groups is also important. It allows you to stress important values and behaviours. *'I would like to say thank you to whoever it was, he went the extra mile and showed such kindness in digging a colleague's car out of the snow.'* My favourite way of saying thank you is what I call the 'three-fold thanks', and I use this at significant moments such as promotion, retirement or other achievements. *'Thank you for all your work on […], thank you for your outstanding contribution to our school and thank you for all you are. It is a privilege to work with you.'* The beauty of the rule of three is that you can thank colleagues for different things and emphasise different areas of their work. It must, however, flow and should always be heartfelt.

Saying *'thank you'* creates small waves of appreciation and ripples of gratitude. A culture of appreciation and feeling valued can stem from simply saying *'thank you'*. New leaders should say *'thank you'* with authenticity. This makes colleagues feel useful and appreciated.

> *Be polite and say, 'thank you', well. Make colleagues feel useful and appreciated.*

REFLECTION QUESTION

How have leaders made you feel useful and appreciated?

TASKS

1. Add a qualifying why, every time you say thank you.
2. Imagine one of your closest colleagues is about to retire. You give a leaver's speech. Identify the three things that you are thanking them for. Say this clearly and with authenticity.
3. Can you do this for every colleague in your team?

Chapter 25
QUESTIONS

Everyone says that I ask a lot of questions. Yesterday I received my Covid-19 vaccination. It took far longer than I thought. I sat in the booth, reading the signs and medical information, whilst waiting for the nurse. A question then popped into my mind about the potential side effects, and I decided that I ought to find out the answer. The GP needed to be called, but wasn't available as someone had fainted. A senior nurse and then pharmacist came to answer the question and finally asked if I had any more questions – '*no*'. I knew my wife was experiencing a much longer delay than she expected because of me and she would be waiting for me in the car. The medical team were all smiling, satisfied that they had dealt with this curious patient. Now, I waited calmly for the jab. Maybe I ask too many questions. I ask questions all day, seeking understanding, but maybe I need to learn when to stop.

Teachers have long understood the importance of questioning in learning. Indeed, they talk about Socratic questioning to seek understanding, provoke discussion, challenge assumptions and analyse arguments. But am I naturally curious and an asker of questions or does leadership drive me to ask questions?

There are many types of questions, but there are three that work best for me – questions that I use regularly throughout the day.

The opener. I find this question to be useful in all one-to-one meetings. You can play around with how you phrase the question, but essentially you ask, *'what are you thinking?'*, *'what is on your list?'*, *'what is on your mind?'*. This usually instigates a flow of information.

The seeker. We must use this type of question within the context of trust and positivity. Ask with the aim of understanding ideas or the reason something has happened. *The seeker* allows you to hear colleagues explain their thoughts, revealing their logic and shining a light on the root cause of an issue. I use *'explain how?'* and *'explain why?'*. For example, *'explain how this will have an impact?'*, *'explain why this has happened?'* or *'why are you thinking this?'*. *The seeker* leads you to the truth, almost.

The revealer. We must only use this type of question after *the opener* and *the seeker*. Use this to refine ideas, conclude a discussion or unlock a new direction of the discussion. My favourite *revealer* questions are *'what do you want?'*, *'what is the actual issue?'*, *'what have we decided?'*, *'what next?'* or *'what else?'*. It is tempting to start these questions with *'so'*, but I think the questioning sounds more confident if you sound the *'so'* in your mind, rather than saying it aloud.

With all these questions, I have learnt to say the question precisely. I then simply pause, nod and continue to pause. The pause is as important as the question itself, inviting the space for your colleagues to speak. You must then listen with humility and respect for their ideas, and most importantly with curiosity. Asking a question and listening is one of the most important things that a new leader can do. I continue to ask lots of questions. Questions help you connect, help you to seek new ideas and help you to reveal underlying thinking.

> *Asking questions helps you connect, seek new ideas and reveal underlying thinking. Do this precisely, pause and listen with curiosity.*

REFLECTION QUESTION

What questions do you ask colleagues? Are they effective? Do you listen?

TASKS

1. Write *'opener, seeker and revealer'* in your notebook or on a piece of paper.
2. In your next meeting, follow the questioning order of *'opener, seeker and revealer'*.
3. Remember to pause and listen well.

Chapter 26

VISITS

I remember my first school trip to the fire station. The pole was so shiny, and we were all allowed to slide from the top-floor staffroom to the ground floor where the fire engines were kept. The engine was the finest shade of red. We returned to school and wrote about our day. We chatted about the visit with our friends and family, and we drew on the experience in our play. Visits foster learning and we shouldn't forget their importance as new leaders.

We have a brilliant scheme where a colleague joins our senior leadership team for the week. I like colleagues joining the team and hope that their visit will resonate with them. At the end of the week, I ask what they gained from their experience, how we could be more efficient, whether our roles could be clearer and if they have any ideas about how we could improve. There seems to be a reciprocal benefit to visits if you act towards your guests with openness and humility.

I spoke with an experienced headteacher with the idea to pair our senior colleagues and carry out an exchange visit. We were both preparing for an Ofsted inspection, but we also just wanted to generate ideas. There is always a very special moment during visits where you take what you see and apply this to your own setting. It makes me smile when I walk into our sixth form where we have pictures of previous pupils and words that describe *'what it takes to be successful'* – a simple idea taken from a visit. I knew that this next visit would lead to the sharing of ideas, collaboration and new thinking. Discussing and sharing with others creates a zone of creativity where you can push forward with new ideas.

During my walkabout visits around the school, I try to visit parts of the school I don't always go to. This week I visited the office next door, just for a few minutes, because some areas are too easy to miss. It was interesting to ask about their work, what issues they face and how we could improve. We laughed together and my visit connected me to my colleagues.

A few years ago, I visited a partner school in Switzerland. Just seeing the school inspired me to take pictures of their classrooms and artwork to share with colleagues. I learnt a brief speech in French, and forged new links that led to exchange visits for pupils.

Visits are a lesson in themselves about leadership. Leadership isn't about control and sitting still; leadership is about collaboration, sharing of ideas and restlessness to learn from others. Visits give perspective, and leaders need to refresh their perspective. Visits give us ideas and a picture of something different, just as they did a child at the fire station.

Seize any opportunity to carry out a visit, relentlessly learning from others.

REFLECTION QUESTION

You need perspective and new ideas: who and where can you visit?

TASKS

1. Identify a part of the school you never or rarely visit. Go and see it.
2. Seek best practice and innovation in other schools or organisations and visit with members of your team. Forge dialogue and enjoy the zone of creativity.
3. Then arrange reciprocal visits – there is always a washback effect that benefits others.

Chapter 27

FEEDBACK

People say things in interviews that often reveal their values, inner thinking and overall attitudes. Sometimes this goes well, sometimes less well. Today, everything fell on the side of going less well. I asked the candidate to reflect on how well his trial lesson had gone. He told me it had gone well, but he *'could just tell that the boy in front of him was low ability'*. The words struck me, and I replayed them in my mind. He used the phrase again, then again. I couldn't take it anymore, so I asked him if he could *'just tell'*, when he entered my office for his interview, out of the three of us on the panel, which one of us was of low ability? Maybe this wasn't the kindest of reactions, but I felt compelled to act. We hear, read and face many interesting scenarios as new leaders, so we must form our own relationship with feedback; how we receive feedback and how we give feedback.

I have learnt to welcome both personal and organisational feedback, seeing it as an opportunity to implement positive change. This isn't always straightforward, as we can receive feedback that we don't wish to see or hear. Often, feedback feels overly personal, especially when we feel the values of the organisation are so closely aligned to our own – what they say about the organisation feels like what they are saying about me. Often leaders obsess about details, perfecting procedures and routines, so the feedback cuts. A painful blow, preventing us from seeing the opportunity to improve.

Giving feedback seems so much easier and less complex than receiving it, especially if you have a clear set of organisational values such as *'honesty'* or *'excellence'*. That said, I try to stick to the following principles.

Don't delay. If you feel that feedback needs to be given, positive or negative, then do it straight away. This makes the feedback relevant.

Make it clear. If you have something that needs to be said, it needs to be stated clearly. Make sure they understand in no uncertain terms. You shouldn't shroud the message in apology or make it overly complex. Cut to the chase and make feedback easily understood.

Do it yourself, do it kindly, but also with confidence. I have learnt that asking others to give feedback on your behalf serves only to create the impression of cowardice or create confusion from second-hand communication. Take responsibility as a leader and give feedback yourself. Do this kindly and with confidence. Often it is much easier than you think, as most people have a reasonable understanding of their own behaviour. A few open questions often lead them to a place of reflection. Make sure you express your point of view with confidence.

New leaders must develop an effective relationship with feedback. With kindness, confidence, clarity and without delay, the interviewee who *'could just tell that the boy in front of me was low ability'* received feedback about his performance. He already understood, he could *'just tell'*.

> *Give feedback without delay and make it clear. Do it yourself, do it kindly but also with confidence.*

REFLECTION QUESTION

How do you seek and give feedback?

TASKS

1. Think of examples where you have given feedback that hasn't gone well. Can this be explained by delay, lack of clarity, not doing it yourself or lack of confidence? Were any other factors at play?
2. Identify all the ways you give and receive feedback. Are opportunities being missed?
3. What new avenues of feedback could you explore?

Chapter 28
NEXT STEPS

Everyone stopped to look. Slowly and cautiously, he stepped forward, balanced and stepped again. Each step was a little more confident than the last. With each step, his smile grew stronger. He realised how others were reacting. *'Look, look, he's doing it, he's walking'*, my father said.

There is something inherently moving about watching your child take their first steps. The memory of my son, Tristan, making his first steps, is poignant for me. I saw his first steps with my brother and father before my dad's sudden death. Thinking about my son's first steps and the reaction of loved ones reminds me of the special link between leadership and steps.

When I think about the next steps, ask about the next steps or make my own next steps, I am recreating something of the beauty of that moment – that moment when an intention turns into action and when the expectation becomes a reality. We must learn to be interested in *next steps* as leaders.

Asking about *'the next step'* is a simple and purposeful way of clarifying what needs to happen. I have sat through many meetings, scribbling in my notebook, attempting to fathom the action and next steps. I have learnt to pause routinely in a meeting and ask, *'what are the next steps?'* Even better, I ask someone to summarise them. I have learnt to ask myself this question when I observe a teacher or meet with a colleague, *'what is the next step to help them?'* It makes the changes needed much clearer.

When I meet with a parent, I find this question helps to simplify what needs to be done to effect a change. When I walk through the school, I ask *'what is the next step?'*, which helps me to focus on how we can improve the school for our pupils.

Next steps thinking and questioning drives change, hopefully in the agreed right direction. It also helps leaders in any situation to embrace moments of crisis. Thinking in this way helps you to pause and work through the best next step.

When reflecting on my performance and thinking about how I can improve, I drive this by working out the next step. However tricky or tentative the next step needs to be, this thinking moves me forward. *Next steps* thinking sets up action; an expectation that can become a reality.

It is a false assumption, however, to think that the next best step is always forward. Sometimes there are hazards and traps in front of us that can cause easy falls. Sometimes we need to step to the side and let someone else step forward. Sometimes we need to step back and take some more time or explore a different route. Sometimes we need to step back, sidestep and then step forward. It is important, therefore, to avoid being fooled by the *fallacy of always stepping forward*.

The importance of stepping up or stepping down similarly confirms the ridiculousness of the *fallacy of stepping forward*. I have learnt that colleagues can develop significantly from stepping up – *'take over for a moment and lead the meeting'* or stepping down *'this doesn't work, and you need to take a different path'*. The ability and humility to recognise that your behaviour or job is simply not working requires a clarity of thinking that the *fallacy of stepping forward* can conceal.

Thinking about the *next steps* makes new leaders productive and purposeful. But recognise that not all steps are equal, and some steps involve more danger and fear than others, whatever the direction. Think deeply about the *next steps* and remember the moment children take the first couple of steps that became more confident steps. The simple power of refining leads to progress.

When I saw my son take his first steps, intending to walk, and my parental expectation became reality, I forgot about the many stepping stones that helped him on his way. The holding of hands, the gentle catching, the careful balancing act of parenting. We must remember we often need stepping stones to make the next step. Whilst leadership is about *next steps*, and this can make you very productive, don't forget the stepping stones we need to gift others as leaders.

> *Next steps thinking drives action. Be mindful that stepping forward is not always the best next step.*

REFLECTION QUESTION

How do you apply next steps thinking in your school?

TASKS

1. What is the fallacy of stepping forward?
2. List examples of when stepping forward is not the best next step.
3. Why is next steps thinking so impactful?

Chapter 29

THE GIFT OF HELPING OTHERS TO CROSS STEPPING STONES

The Tour de Mont Blanc is a 120-mile walk that encompasses the whole of the Mont Blanc Massif, taking you through forests, moraines and the mountains of France, Switzerland and Italy. I didn't know it then, but this walk, with my tent and rucksack, was an important lesson in stepping stones. After finishing my degree, I caught the Eurolines coach from Victoria Station in London to Chamonix. I was travelling with a friend I met in my university hall of residence. Like me, he had finished his studies and wanted to travel to Europe.

The journey on the coach was long, hot and uncomfortable and we were keen to set off as soon as we arrived in Chamonix. With the dramatic scenery of the snow-covered alps against a bright blue sky, I felt the weight of my rucksack as beads of sweat formed and trickled down my face.

By day three, I could feel soreness in my feet and the tiredness of sleeping in a tent that was always going to be a compromise between weight and space. But something wasn't right. We arrived tired in Courmayeur and my friend turned to me and said, '*I have had enough, I don't like it, I'm going back to London*'.

Within 30 minutes, he had found a bus and was gone. I felt no resentment, but I did feel that I really ought to think about what I had better do next.

I thought it best to let my parents know of my intention to walk alone. I heard the familiar voice of my mum on the phone and listened to her gentle understanding. She then said, *'I'll just put Dad on'*. With very few words, he gave me a lesson on helping others to make the next move – a very clear and positive stepping stone placed in front of me. He simply said, *'you can do it, no problem'*. And, despite the challenge of many miles walking alone, I made it back, *'no problem'*.

There is something inherently encouraging in knowing that the significant others in your life have belief in you. It simply gives you the confidence to try.

I try to remember the vital message of helping people to cross stepping stones. I find it interesting to look at colleagues and imagine them crossing a river, thinking about how they would cross, how they would react when the stone wobbled and how they would behave if the next step were a bigger and more dangerous stretch.

Leaders create opportunities for people, stepping stones in their careers. By inviting colleagues to apply for a new role or inviting them to step up and lead an initiative, we are saying to them *'you can do it, no problem'*. By asking someone to be a coach, lead an investigation or complete an advanced course, we are implicitly telling them, *'you can do it, no problem'*.

How a colleague reacts reflects their confidence and motivation as much as their faith in you. For some, the stepping stone is too far away and too frightening a step to make. In this situation, I ask if I have done everything I can to explain what the step will be like and if have I helped enough. If that doesn't work, I forget and think of an alternative step. I remember how rewarding it will be when they successfully make the step and cross.

When leaders help colleagues across stepping stones, they gift a sense that says, '*I believe in you*'. Leaders should then relinquish control, empowering others with their trust. Letting them take responsibility and develop themselves.

Create stepping stones. Empower others to take responsibility and develop themselves.

REFLECTION QUESTION

How often do you say to others '*you can do it, no problem*'?

TASKS

1. For each of your colleagues, note the stepping stone you want to create for them.
2. If you are not able to do this for all colleagues, why not?
3. On a continuum of easy to difficult, do you find it easy or difficult to relinquish control and empower others with your trust? What steps could you take to change this?

Chapter 30
THE IMPORTANCE OF PREPARATION

The narrative we learn about leadership tells us that the leader lights up the room. Their charisma inspires action, the room feels their presence and people flock to the leader. I don't see myself as that kind of leader. I do, however, want to have gravitas. I want to be convincing in my role. I want others to know how seriously I take it and show how much respect I give the role. By leading well, I understand that this creates feelings of trust in others.

The entire staff stood in the round in front of me as I led the briefing. Traditionally, the headteacher starts the briefing and shares important messages, thanks and praise. The headteacher then asks, *'any messages for today?'*, colleagues raise their hands in turn and we work around the room, for no good reason, in an anti-clockwise direction. The individuals who speak talk with confidence and humour and present their message with flow. I have stuttered and grunted my way through briefings with my very own brand of awkwardness.

Once, my mind simply blanked – nothing, just for a few moments, that awful feeling of choking. I have called colleagues by the wrong name and awkwardly tried to recover. Another time, I mentioned that a colleague was to be married during the holiday and that we had a card and gift for them. I then walked into the middle of the room as did they to collect their card; I lowered myself from my 6 foot 4 inch height to kiss them on the cheek – sadly, my timing was out, and I delivered the peck smack on the lips.

Leaders need to take responsibility when they fall short – most people make mistakes, appear awkward from time to time, and sometimes simply get it wrong. When we think of why this happens, we often fall into the trap of making excuses – '*I wasn't ready*', '*I didn't have time to prepare*', '*I didn't think*'.

One of the reasons for these mistakes sits comfortably at the door, however, of not being prepared. We must take responsibility to reduce these mistakes from happening. And this is an important step if new leaders wish to preserve gravitas.

Embarrassment may drive your thoughts inwards, and experiences, when you make mistakes, provide a useful point of reflection. If I make a mistake, I know full well what I think of myself. I then ask, '*how do others perceive me?*' and '*how do I want to be perceived?*'. One positive learning from these *mistakes of presentation* is to ask whether there was anything you could have done to avoid this by being more organised and prepared. And the answer is, probably, yes.

I have learnt three techniques to make sure that I am prepared. First, I adopt the rule of never ever trying to free-style public speaking. In whatever form it may take, I prepare fully my words and, whilst I might appear to be speaking freely, you hear something planned and measured. Second, I avoid making excuses for time. My calendar governs my day at work, and I allocate *time to tasks* and not just *time to meetings*. This gives me the time to think, plan and ensure that I am prepared. Third, I pause. I pause throughout the day to glance at my calendar for the next hour, the afternoon, the following day, the week ahead and the month ahead. This forces me to think ahead and prepare. It protects me from the pitfall of simply not being ready.

Ethnomethodology is a branch of sociology, developed by Howard Garfinkel, to help understand '*people methods*'. It focuses on how people construct their worlds by trying to make sense of others in everyday situations they encounter. Much of this is based on what he called common sense *taken for granted assumptions* that we hold; giving a red rose to someone takes no explanation of what this means. Garfinkel (1967) went on to describe how we also fill in the gaps with meaning to make sense of the world. A headteacher, for example, wearing a pair of tracksuit bottoms is helping with PE, and probably not someone having a personal crisis showing up to work in the wrong trousers. A headteacher who is prepared and organised is likely to be someone who takes their role seriously and who therefore has gravitas.

It is useful for new leaders to remember that colleagues make sense of the behaviours leaders display. If I keep my desk tidy, if I always look the part and if I arrive prepared and present with clarity, people will perceive me as the leader that I want to be. They fill in the gaps – he must work hard and he is always calm.

Organisation and preparation are non-negotiable for leaders. Give it the attention it needs as people will do the rest in their perception of you – probably as someone with gravitas.

Organisation and preparation are non-negotiable for leaders.

REFLECTION QUESTION

How do leaders create the impression of gravitas?

TASKS

1. List the mistakes of preparation that you have made. What should you have done differently?
2. What steps could you take to develop your gravitas as a leader?

Chapter 31
MEETINGS

Meetings play an important role in the life of a leader. We spend many hours in them, often at the request of others. A minefield of time-wasting, poor planning and costly low productivity. With your time all blocked up in them and a small amount of other time allocated to follow-up action, you realise you must approach meetings with intentionality. The aim must be simple – to halt time saboteurs, make meetings worthwhile and avoid unnecessary ones. New leaders must conquer and master meetings. And by adopting some key principles and understanding the complexity of the interplay of the principles, new leaders can take comfort that their meetings are effective.

The complexity of meetings shouldn't surprise us. Interactions with one another can be hard enough, but layer that with more people, with different views, values and goals, and we have a recipe for social disaster. My starting point with meetings is to adopt a humble stance based on the *Lake Wobegon Effect* – the human tendency to overestimate your ability. We spend so much time in meetings, serving time sat down, that we mistake experience for expertise. We easily fall into a trap of thinking we perform better in meetings than we do. Adopting a humble position and seeking to evaluate the performance of others in meetings is crucial. Here are my principles for meetings with teams.

Principle one: make others the priority

Principle one dictates you must *make others the priority*. You must select the right people for the meeting and the right number of people. Ten is about the maximum number for decision-making. Base the meeting on evidence with ideally one-page proposals or a one-page research summary that someone has prepared. If you need a longer report, it must be read in advance by all. Now chair the meeting, making others the priority. Give them space to speak. Let others lead by closing your mouth.

Principle two: you must avoid distractions

Principle two states that *you must avoid distractions*. The quality of your written agenda, with identified intended outcomes, an outline of the meeting process and clear time allocation, helps to keep you on track. But mobile phones, side conversations, permitted interruptions and lack of direction cause drift. This also violates principle one because wasting people's time is not making them the priority. Make time your ally or fall into an alleyway of diversion, interference and hindrance.

Principle three: effective time management

Principle three demands *effective time management*. When we meet with others, we can work together and forge collective solutions. But we can also simply waste time. Swiss trains run on time because it matters that they run on time. Because you are exercising the privilege of using the time of others, it matters that meetings run on time. Whistles signify the train is going to set off; use markers in the meeting to signpost discussion time, decision time or the next step of the meeting.

Be prepared to bring the meeting to a close if productivity is low and rearrange with the right people in the room. And never forget *Parkinson's Law*. Work will fill the time you allocate, so be kind and arrange one-hour meetings for 50 minutes, and 30-minute meetings for 25 minutes. Time is a gift, so avoid wasting the time of others at all costs.

Principle four: avoid bias

Principle four dictates that you must *avoid bias*. Bias takes many forms and amounts to distortion. Leaders must check their own influence, control their mood and present themselves as level-headed and balanced. I find it useful to seek first the views of others, before offering my own, so I don't falsely steer the thinking of the group. Asking others to write their thoughts or idea before a discussion also mitigates bias.

Select your seating position carefully, at the centre of the long side of a rectangle table, not at the head, with colleagues then in the round, to reduce awarding an individual a privileged position where they dominate.

Principle five: foster positive conflict and forge effective participation

We must regulate the behaviour of others through principle five, which states you must *foster positive conflict and forge effective participation*. Effective meetings need trust within the team to encourage divergent viewpoints. Foster a climate where different views are welcome and where robust challenge is the norm. Chair this with care because ridicule, sarcasm, the shaking of heads and fighting for space to talk by interrupting others are just examples of permitted rudeness. Set the tone and don't let this happen.

Lots of talking doesn't mean a good meeting. You can create effective participation by using silence to give space to think, for colleagues to write their own views and use silent reading to generate further questions. Know how your colleagues behave in meetings, who holds back and who dives in. Know when to bring others in and draw on the skills and views of all participants.

Principle six: seek agreement but recognise when to direct

Principle six takes practice and a good deal of listening; it demands that leaders *seek agreement but recognise when to direct*. There is always a point in a meeting, a unique moment of synergy, where the collective discussion of the group reveals an agreement. Be ready for this moment, step in and summarise the outcome or decision. On some agenda items that unique point is harder to find, and in these moments leaders should direct and nudge things along. Sometimes you dislike the direction of the meeting, and the beauty of leadership is that you can direct it. In this scenario, you need to offer a concise explanation, drawing on the points already made, about why you are not prepared to go in this direction. Then, state the direction and open the discussion again.

Sometimes the meeting can't reach a conclusion because more information is needed. Be ready to stop the meeting at this point and return when you have everything you need.

Principle seven: evaluate every meeting

The ultimate principle pulls all the principles together and recognises the complexity of meetings. Principle seven requires leaders to *evaluate every meeting*. You can do this quickly at the end of the meeting, asking someone to summarise whether the meeting has been a good use of time. A different option is to use a meeting evaluation form, asking colleagues to summarise their own performance and contribution, what they gained from the meeting and if there is anything they wanted to say but didn't.

Inviting other colleagues to observe the meeting is also a good way to challenge your own perceptions. Ask them to consider if roles were clear, if any time was wasted, if people contributed equally and if there was any perceived bias. Avoid the *Lake Wobegon Effect*.

Meetings take different forms – walking meetings, huddles, one-to-ones, briefings and decision-making meetings – and provide a unique opportunity to unleash the collective power of others by working together. Meetings take time and practice to master, especially ones with seven to ten colleagues in your team who work so closely together. You need to use all seven principles to make them work. One-to-one meetings need a lighter touch in terms of the principles. Your entire focus should be on making the other person the priority.

We should respect the power of meetings like the world's best climbers learn to respect the mountains or the world's best surfers respect the sea. With effective stewarding, using the seven principles, meetings have the power to be highly productive, but they can quickly deteriorate and be much less impactful.

And then there is the '*Any Other Business*' hand grenade lob, where someone raises an issue with only five minutes left. There are different ways to prevent this. Plan your agendas well in advance by listening to others with care so that all the most difficult items are already included. This simply removes the need for the AOB lob. If a new AOB hand grenade still comes up, you can choose to hold it so that it doesn't explode. Simply catch it and decide what you want to do with it. I suggest that you throw it straight out of the room.

> *Master the seven principles of effective meetings: make others the priority, avoid distractions, effectively manage time, avoid bias, foster positive conflict, seek agreement and evaluate every meeting.*

REFLECTION QUESTION

Why are meetings so often unproductive?

TASKS

1. How effective are you in chairing meetings or participating in them?
2. Invite a colleague to observe one of your meetings. Ask them to consider whether all roles were clear, whether any time was wasted, whether people contributed equally and whether there was any perceived bias in your approach.
3. Introduce a method so participants can evaluate their own performance in your meeting. Ask them to summarise their own performance and contribution, what they gained from the meeting and ask them if there is anything they wanted to say but didn't.

Chapter 32

READING

The doorbell rang. I opened the door, and the postal worker handed me a large bundle of envelopes containing exam scripts. He laughed and said, *'that's not all mate'* and passed me two more bundles. An experienced teacher had talked to me about how useful it would be to work for the exam board, marking exam papers. Newly qualified and keen to learn, I duly signed up with the exam board. I carried the packages inside and piled them high on my desk. I looked at them and thought, *'lots of reading'*.

I remember how nervous I was about marking those first few scripts. Despite working for the exam board for many years, I never failed to worry about passing the sample that had to be checked by a senior examiner before you were allowed to mark. Marking exam papers every night teaches you something about the capacity of the brain to handle large volumes of words. I must have read thousands and thousands of handwritten pages. I learnt to read in pockets of time, with focus, at a steady pace, holding the information in my mind, working out what the candidate was trying to say whilst trying to apply a mark scheme fairly. Exam board marking allowed me to practise and develop my reading.

In sixth form, a teacher told me to read *Wild Swans* by Jung Chang (1992) and then Nelson Mandela's (1995) *Long Walk to Freedom*. I remember being daunted by the length of the books but I read a little every day until I became hooked. Their voices slowly took a form in my mind, educating me about worlds different from my own. At university, I fought with how much of the essential and additional reading list you should read before settling on just reading for two hours every day.

I continue to develop as a reader in my role as a new school leader. My reading folder is always full, and I battle to keep up. I sometimes make mistakes when I read, missing words and failing to understand. My errors become so obvious after rereading them aloud. I have never understood speed reading – my reading rhythm is my reading rhythm.

I have learnt that there are different ways to read as a leader. I read widely for information and understanding. Internal reports, wider research and journal articles all provide sources of information, and opportunities to understand and spark ideas. I have learnt to stand back, similar to reading an exam script, and ask *'what is this trying to say?'*. This is important when understanding, for example, the meaning behind a letter of complaint or in the daily exchange of messages between colleagues.

To question the source and check for bias is another thing I have learned. I recognise that others interpret the same text differently and that it is important to check I understand. I have learnt that sometimes people who we think should write well don't. During the pandemic, there was a piece of guidance about how many pupils could return to school. The text was so confusing that I phoned my daughter to ask for her help. A fresh pair of eyes to help me understand.

I am careful about what and how I read. I try to read all the relevant documents that pass across my desk. I glance through Twitter and try to keep up to date with education press and journal articles. I read most of the newspaper on a Sunday morning and finish it during the week. I try to read a wider leadership book each month and have a fiction book on the go. I am kind to myself, recognising that, like the additional reading list at university, I can't read everything.

There is so much to read as a new leader that the only way to cope is to make reading a regular part of your routine. Take care of what you read so that you have the most valid inputs for the profession. Take care of how you read so that you fully understand. Try to read critically on the side of understanding, recognising that your truth is just that, your own constructed understanding. Read widely as a new leader, fostering ideas and forging understanding.

Make reading part of your routine. Read widely, fostering ideas and forging understanding.

REFLECTION QUESTION

What are you reading to help you develop as a new school leader?

TASKS

1. Is reading part of your routine?
2. When reading reports, correspondence, or complaints, ask, what is each source trying to say?
3. Is the source valid and does it contain bias? Are you reading critically on the side of understanding, recognising that your truth is just that, your own constructed understanding?
4. See the recommended reading at the end.

Chapter 33

CARRYING ON

'People are just worn-out, Neil.'

The last week of term always ends in this way. Standing back, watching and listening, it is easy to spot a narrative of declining energy levels and people just needing to stop. But how do new leaders carry on?

At this point in the term, I try to remind myself of visits to Brighouse, a small market town in Calderdale, West Yorkshire. My grandma would sit, often reading in her chair before making tea, always with the same colourful teapot and always with a serving of shortbread biscuits. As my mum chatted with her, my brother would begin his ritual of finding the one screwdriver in the kitchen and dissembling a metal stool – a white one with a wooden seat. At first, I would observe my big brother in awe and wonder as he performed this feat of engineering. Having observed this deconstruction and reconstruction many times and knowing that he would succeed in this act, I began my very own ritual. I liked to quietly leave the room and look at my grandma's bed – a bed with no legs. I would sit in wonder at her bed that was propped up, perfectly level, with stacks of books, instead of legs.

Growing up after the First World War, and then bringing up your own children during the Second World War, must shape you. Her bed with no legs expressed what she learnt in her early life. There is always a solution. You can adapt and you can carry on. Whenever we described a challenge that we faced, she would reply *'it will pass'*, and whenever an opportunity came her way – a bus ride, a chance to win a raffle, a drive to the Yorkshire Dales – she would say *'count me in'*.

Other people *'finishing their work off'* characterises the last week of term. They achieve this by passing their work to colleagues: rushed letters needing to be sent out on their behalf or a last-minute call to a parent. My email inbox fills, and I flag the important ones like a mountain climber striking their axe into ice. The workload always intensifies – a crescendo to a finale, just with a tired mind. But new leaders must still lead. And when things get difficult and tiring, they need to draw on something to carry on.

I have learnt to draw on my learning from Brighouse when I approach the last week. Facing an unstoppable rush, I try to shift to a particular mindset – the *grandma mindset*. I see the week as something that *will pass*. It will end. Because of this, I approach every difficulty as a challenge, despite how I feel, and say *'count me in'*. This keeps me positive, interested and productive. I think of my brother taking the stool apart and putting it back together. I can see in my mind the scratches of use on the wooden seat and can hear him say, *'sit on it, it still works'*. This reminds me that things can be reset – work will get back to normal. I think of a bed with no legs, held up by books. This makes me smile. I might not fully complete all my work, but there is always a solution to get you through to the end of term.

> *Busy times will pass, so approach every difficulty as a challenge, staying curious and positive.*

REFLECTION QUESTION

How do you perceive challenge at the very end of a busy term?

TASKS

1. Identify why your workload intensifies at the end of each term.
2. What steps can you take to address this if it is outside of your control?
3. What mindset can you adopt to lead more effectively when you simply need to find the inner strength to carry on?

Chapter 34

RESTART

In 1993, I was in Year 9. My teacher used to be a PE teacher but now taught geography as he aged in the profession. Wearing a brown suit and a silver pair of glasses, he was friendly and kind. I remember his black bag because it had three initials written on it and I could see the initials from where I used to sit. I used to try to work out his first and middle name.

I think about him at the start of each term because he used to repeat the same thing. He would say, *'don't worry now about the last term, if you did badly, if you did well, it's now time to restart'*.

'It is now time to restart.' I like this message. However difficult something has been, whether I succeeded or whether I failed, whether I tried my best or didn't, I can *'restart'* and be different, *'restart'* and improve, *'restart'* and develop. Leaders too can *'restart'*.

After the pandemic, I attended a Burns Night celebration at school. The event raises lots of money for sports at the school through the generous donations of raffle prizes from local businesses. I paid 20 pounds to one of the pupil volunteers selling tickets and thought nothing more of the raffle, knowing I never win. The evening ended and I noticed a member of the PTA smiling at me with a glint in their eye. Surprised, I asked, 'what's happened?'. 'Mr Renton, you've won,' they said. 'What have I won?' 'A six-week total body transformation at the gym in town.'

Elated about my new experience of raffle victory, it took a while to understand the reality of my prize. My wife adopted a firm, slightly intimidating approach that said, *'you will commit to this transformation'*. Colleagues smiled at the thought that a headteacher, clearly failing to exercise through the pandemic, could transform himself through high-intensity interval training.

This, however, was my victory, and in a quiet moment I phoned the number on the prize envelope and enquired about what this would involve. Could six weeks of training transform me?

I summoned up the courage and spoke to the coach, who struck me with enthusiasm and positivity, encouraging me to dig out my trainers and just *'come on down'*.

I found myself in a bright gym with TV screens on the wall, perfectly arranged equipment and people who clearly knew what they were doing. The demo then started.

The coaches showed you how to do the activity and the TV screens also displayed each move. Then it started.

'60 seconds work – 30 seconds rest – move – two circuits – then 30 seconds work – 20 seconds rest.' I needed to concentrate; this was a new world for me. The coach recognised my fear and gave kind words of reassurance.

In time, I would learn how to burpee, lunge, squat, sumo squat, hand walk, dead ball slam and ice skate. From the moment of the first beep, signifying that it is now time to move, the coaches gave me the confidence to try. Swinging a kettlebell for the first time whilst lunging to the side, somewhat short of breath, I thought, how similar great teaching is to what I was experiencing.

At school, we have spent time researching the very best ways for children to learn based on the latest research in brain science.

My new coaches were following the research to the letter, delivered with passion and enthusiasm:

- connecting with me at the start, with positivity, to engage; delivering simple and clear teacher instructions in small steps to minimise cognitive overload;
- modelling what I needed to do, but adapting the moves so that everyone can achieve success;
- letting me crack on and providing me with challenge;
- giving feedback, and coaching, straight away so that I could improve.

I then approached a long pole – the revo bar – and thought about how well organised my experience was. The regime involved a well-thought-out, sequenced curriculum allowing me to do more. No one can escape the exercise.

The coaches gave me the confidence to exercise and try something new. They showed patience. In every session, they steered me in the right direction, encouraged and pushed me.

After six weeks of training four times a week, I felt 100 per cent fitter. I lost weight, felt stronger, slept better and put stress from the day neatly away in a box. During the pandemic I would have never imagined myself being in a gym, being so wrapped up in the moment of completing a workout that instead of the single fist bump etiquette at the end of the session, I dived straight in with a double fist bump.

My old geography teacher and the coaches taught me a very simple lesson. You can restart, you can reset and you can be different.

> *However difficult something has been, whether you have succeeded or whether you have failed, you can restart, reset and be different.*

REFLECTION QUESTION

Is it time to reset and do something differently?

TASKS

1. Identify an experience where your leadership has failed and where your leadership has succeeded.
2. Why is it important to reset after failure and success?
3. Do you have a strategy in place *'to put stress from the day neatly away in a box'*?

Chapter 35

MOMENTS THAT GIVE PERSPECTIVE

I am waiting for the call to board a flight to Warsaw, waiting for when the aeroplane kicks forward and takes off. That moment when the wheels lift into the air. This is the moment in which the previous half term takes perspective. The smallest of spaces between the wheels and the runway are all I need to regain clarity of thought. Even the sight of the wheels against the runway as I climb the stairs to board the plane starts a process in my mind that will soon deliver a moment of perspective.

Moments of perspective exist in different forms. Even in the dark winter months, when people are making their journey home, I like to shut my computer down and tidy my desk. I make the brief journey across my office to the large meeting table and take out my notepad. The scribbles, crossings out and quick notes about the day spread across the page – revealing the pattern of the day. I turn the page and write tomorrow's date in the top right-hand corner. I strike a line under the date. As I write a new list, I feel a new perspective emerge. The simple act of writing a list before I walk home creates space for rest, freeing up the few hours before sleep so I can see clearly again.

I look in front of me and see our dog scurry from the path by the reservoir to the exciting smells of the wood. She glances to check if we are still there. Talking with my wife as we walk helps rationalise my thoughts. Her questions and the story that she creates in her mind leads to more questions and the need for more explanation – a different lens. The fresh air, the smell of the wood and the conversation, discussion and working out of solutions give me a new view. With red cheeks in front of the fire and a contented dog sitting at my side, I have restored my perspective.

Moments of perspective crucially allow us to see things a little more accurately on the arc of truth. The moment of take-off on the plane, writing a list and walking the dog help me to see more effectively. Tomorrow I will wake up in Poland and put the tiredness of the half term behind me – as the proverb says, *'morning is wiser than evening'*. New leaders need to find moments of perspective.

> *Moments of perspective allow you to see things more accurately. Leaders need to find moments of perspective.*

REFLECTION **QUESTION**

Do you create sufficient space to benefit from moments of perspective?

TASKS

1. Identify a time when you believe that you had the most accurate perspective across the arc of truth. What were you doing to reach this moment of perspective?
2. What steps could you take to ensure that you have sufficient rest?
3. Are others around you speaking from a position of moments of perspective? How would you know?

Part 3
SUMMARY

Leading every day requires a commitment to curiosity. This will help you to gain insight from which you build wisdom. Don't worry about where your team works, think more about how you work. Create a time for your team to work collectively, without distraction, on the future direction. In all your work and from the very beginning, remember to smile. This signifies confidence, care and connection. And make colleagues feel useful and appreciated by being polite and saying '*thank you*' well.

One way to satisfy curiosity is to ask questions. This will help you connect, seek new ideas and reveal underlying thinking. Do this precisely, pause and listen with curiosity. Visits also give you the opportunity to learn from others, so seize any opportunity to observe different places of work.

New leaders can develop colleagues by giving feedback without delay and making feedback clear. Do it yourself, do it kindly but also with confidence. A relentless focus on the next steps can drive action and give opportunities to others. Empower others to take responsibility and help them to develop themselves across stepping stones.

We blunder as new leaders and often the root cause is poor organisation and preparation. Make organisation and preparation non-negotiable. Meetings are a potential minefield for new leaders. Master the seven principles of effective meetings: make others the priority, avoid distractions, effectively manage time, avoid bias, foster positive conflict, seek agreement and evaluate every meeting.

New leaders must take on board lots of new information, so reading must become a part of your daily routine. Along with all the other challenges, this can make working life busy. Busy times, however, will pass so approach every difficulty as a challenge, staying curious and positive.

Yet however difficult something has been, whether you have succeeded or whether you have failed, remember that you can restart, reset and be different. Moments of perspective also allow you to see things more accurately. New leaders need to find moments of perspective.

Emma Meadus, headteacher at Coppice Valley Primary School, reminds us of the importance of connecting with teams, being visible and being curious about the community you serve.

The basics of leading everyday involve practical steps you can take to answer the question *'what do I do now?'*. Leading every day, however, also requires having the right mindset and creating a positive culture.

Part 3 Case study

Emma Meadus on leading every day: the basics

Leader	Emma Meadus
Setting	Coppice Valley Primary School, Red Kite Learning Trust, Harrogate – primary school of 200 pupils
Role	Headteacher

If you could give two pieces of advice to a new school leader on the basics of leading every day, what would you say?	Be visible, every day. It is easy to get stuck behind your desk all day responding to emails, calls and paperwork. Although these jobs are important, it is vital that you are seen by your school community as a hands-on and present leader, and you need to gather information about how your school works with your own eyes. Walk the school once a day and meet and greet your families as often as you can each week. It will pay dividends in building relationships, trust and respect and knowing the school you are leading. Check in with your staff. It's not possible to speak to every member of staff every day but try to connect with some different staff each and every day to ask how they are and how things are going. This allows you to get a feel for how the individuals are in your school and what systems may or may not be working well. Gathering informal insights into your staff's opinions, well-being and workload issues give you an opportunity to make strategic and operational adaptations to keep the ship on course.
What is the most important leadership book to you?	Scott, K (2017) *Radical Candor: Be a Kick-Ass Boss Without Losing Your Humanity*. New York: St Martin's Press.
Why is this book important?	Kim Scott gives practical advice about how to communicate honestly and effectively with your team to get the culture and results you want.

Give one piece of leadership advice to new school leaders.	Be curious and interested. Get to know all the different groups in your school community – children, parents, staff, governors, but also the neighbours, local businesses and volunteer groups. Spend quality time really understanding how all these groups see your school and what they want from you as a leader.

Part 3 Key points

Leading every day: the basics

1. Unleash curiosity, helping you to gain insight from which you build understanding. Do this positively and with praise to create a purposeful collective conscience.
2. Create a time for your team to work collectively, without distraction, on the future direction.
3. Smiling signifies confidence, care and connection. Remember to do it from the very beginning in your new role and every day.
4. Be polite and say, *'thank you'*, well. Make colleagues feel useful and appreciated.
5. Asking questions helps you connect, seek new ideas and reveal underlying thinking. Do this precisely, pause and listen with curiosity.
6. Seize any opportunity to carry out a visit, relentlessly learning from others.
7. Give feedback without delay and make it clear. Do it yourself, do it kindly but also with confidence.
8. Next steps thinking drives action. Be mindful that stepping forward is not always the best next step.

9. Create stepping stones. Empower others to take responsibility and develop themselves.
10. Organisation and preparation are non-negotiable for leaders.
11. Master the seven principles of effective meetings: make others the priority, avoid distractions, effectively manage time, avoid bias, foster positive conflict, seek agreement and evaluate every meeting.
12. Make reading part of your routine. Read widely, fostering ideas and forging understanding.
13. Busy times will pass, so approach every difficulty as a challenge, staying curious and positive.
14. However difficult something has been, whether you have succeeded or whether you have failed, you can restart, reset and be different.
15. Moments of perspective allow you to see things more accurately. Leaders need to find moments of perspective.

Part 4

LEADING EVERY DAY: MINDSET AND CULTURE

Chapter 36
THE IMPORTANCE OF GOALS

In 2000, studying in my final year at the London School of Economics and determined to do well, I didn't realise then that goals remain constant throughout life. I did well at school and found it difficult to receive the first comment on a piece of work at university, *'this isn't an essay, but a string of sentences'*. At first, I wanted to return North. How could I live in this expensive city at such a cost to my parents when I clearly couldn't hit the mark? Gradually, I improved my performance. With one day off a week to go climbing at Mile End climbing wall and a pint of Guinness in the student union on a Friday, I realised that not only could I achieve, but also keep within a financial budget. I was determined to get a First and the goal made the difference.

That makes it all sound easy, but, worried about my father being made redundant, not being able to focus in a shared room and with distractions in my second year, life seemed to kick away the goal. In January 2000, I visited my friend in Paris. Looking out of the train window from London, I realised goals could become a little hazy as they run away from us. But you can always get them back. Travel and time away often give a lens to better see goals.

When I started my PGCE in London, I was clear that I wanted to become a teacher. I later became a head of department, then an assistant head, then a deputy head, until I became a headteacher. I now want the school to be the best it can be for all children. These goals don't follow me; they are always just in front of me. I don't always like my goals when they seem out of reach, but I can't think of how I would live without them. I know they are my future, past and present.

Goals drive you forward. They prevent distraction, give meaning and create that space, just in front, where success can flourish. New leaders need clear and ambitious goals.

> *Enjoy your relationship with ambitious goals; they prevent distraction, give meaning and create that space, just in front, where success can flourish.*

REFLECTION QUESTION

Simply put, what is your current goal?

TASKS

1. Identify three effective goals that you have achieved in the past.
2. Why did success flourish with these goals?
3. Is your current goal ambitious enough?

Chapter 37

LITTLE THINGS THAT MEAN A LOT

I keep a pack of thank you cards in the bottom left-hand drawer of my desk. It makes me smile when I see them pinned on the wall above the desk of a colleague. Little things mean a lot.

When I was working as a newly appointed head of department, I received a note from the headteacher. Printed on a yellow piece of paper, the note contained three to four sentences of praise. The headteacher had read all my reports for my tutor group and hadn't needed to make a single correction. She wrote to me to say *'well done'* and *'thank you'*. The note made me smile with pride. I took the note home and showed my wife; it caused her to smile. I then showed my mum and the same thing happened. Ten years later I talked with a member of staff who worked with this headteacher long after I had left. She must have continued this note-writing practice and they became known as *'golden memos'*. Little things mean a lot.

I learnt a great deal from this simple human experience of praise and pride. I seize the opportunity to write to colleagues to say thank you. Sometimes it is a simple thank you postcard, on other occasions a longer letter. When staff receive pay progression or go the extra mile, I think it is important that the leader writes meaningful words of praise, recognition and appreciation. When I write these messages, I write from the heart. The emotion of pride is incredibly powerful not only for your own sense of self-worth, but for the culture of the whole organisation. This very fundamental human emotion motivates people, makes people smile and encourages people to be the best they can be.

I often remind myself that little things mean a lot. I thank colleagues at the end of a meeting and say *well done*. If I bump into a member of staff outside of school and they are with their partner or parents, I pay them a compliment and say how privileged I am to work with them. Even out of earshot, this has a powerful effect. They will undoubtedly share the praise. It is contagious and helps foster a positive culture. A little thing that means a lot.

On other occasions, I invite a member of staff or pupil to my office to hear about their achievement, to thank them and say that I am proud of them.

I am naturally quiet and introverted. It has taken me time to become comfortable briefing the whole staff as a new leader. The strategy that helps me to cope with this is to use briefing to praise and kindle the emotion of pride. I don't need to give a fantastic speech or be inspirational. I just need to praise others well. We routinely applaud staff and say a few words of thanks.

All these gestures of praise and pride are small acts of courtesy and recognition that mean a lot. Their power helps establish a positive culture that recognises colleagues.

> *Embrace praise to kindle the emotion of pride. This motivates others through effective recognition.*

REFLECTION QUESTION

How do you create a culture that recognises colleagues?

TASKS

1. What little acts of courtesy and recognition do you use that mean a lot?
2. Do you do this routinely and regularly enough?

Chapter 38
SLOWLY BUILDING TRUST

Feeling ready for a break, I finished work for the half-term holiday. It had been a long spell, with little free time and respite from the pressure. The pandemic had been at its height, and we had kept the school open for vulnerable children and the children of key workers. Learning for the rest of the school had shifted online. Fed up with online meetings and missing the heartbeat of our school, the last week had really tested my leadership. The government said, without much notice or clarity, that schools would reopen for some pupils before the summer holiday.

Earlier in the week, I pulled together my most senior colleagues. We forged a plan. We then presented this plan to the middle leaders. But they really challenged the pace of change and workload. For the first time, I experienced a terrible feeling of losing support and trust. Leadership can be lonely and challenging, but the thought of squandering trust made me feel very low. The phrase *'trust is hard-won, and easily lost'* rattled around my mind. My team rallied, trying to lift me, *'come on, no battle plan survives the first impact'*.

I took some time in the evening after this uncomfortable meeting to think about how to meet the expectations of the government, how to help children and how to keep the goodwill of staff. I keep a notebook next to my bed and, after studying the meeting notes, I scribbled away late into the night. In the morning, things were clearer. We needed to listen to their fears, hear them properly, find solutions to their workload concerns and find an effective compromise. I brought my senior team back together to find solutions to the main issues, and then worked out a more gradual, phased approach.

We arranged an emergency meeting, and we addressed all the concerns and introduced our new adapted plan. Within 48 hours, I felt much calmer and more in control. I hadn't lost trust, and they were with me. I did feel, however, a stronger connection; a tighter bond of trust drawn from humility and listening. I had a plan that was pared back from our original approach, but still a plan that would work and enhance our provision significantly.

I was about to leave the office for the half-term break. I had finished for the day, but I was still in work mode. I glanced at my email and read the following words from a colleague:

> *I would like to send my gratitude for how you and the leadership team are handling the current situation. I can honestly say that the way you have supported and communicated with staff, pupils, and the entire community has been truly remarkable. You have been outstanding with your compassion and guidance, and I feel valued and lucky to be a part of your school.*

The word *'gratitude'* made me pause and draw a breath. Suppose someone had asked, *'what could you do as a new leader to foster gratitude in your team?'*, I genuinely would not have known how to answer that question. Leading through a national crisis with schools closed and where staff miss the camaraderie of work, I have discovered the shadows of an answer. It is not precise but wrapped up in new leaders listening, adapting plans, compromising, communicating, finding solutions to concerns and, above all, showing compassion. I have learnt that there is a close link between honest, wholehearted listening and building trust.

> *Listening, adapting, communicating solutions to concerns and acting with compassion fosters trust and even gratitude.*

REFLECTION QUESTION

What could you do as a new leader to foster gratitude in your team?

TASKS

1. Imagine a time when you try to implement a significant change, but the proposal creates much criticism from staff. You feel that your colleagues have lost trust and faith in you.
2. What steps would you take to address this?
3. How much humility should you show when asked to pare back a plan that you think is the right thing to do?
4. Is there a scenario where you wouldn't listen and implement the plan?

Chapter 39
POSITIVE NARRATIVES

A close friend of mine remembers how her parents, during the Second World War, played games in air-raid shelters as children, how they grew stronger knowing that they could adapt and survive, and how they grew up to appreciate small pleasures. The pain and suffering that they experienced was remarkable, but they adapted and shaped our future.

As a new headteacher in a pandemic, I feared negative narratives such as the *'Covid Generation'*. I didn't understand why anyone would use the term to describe our children. Why would anyone use the name of a disease to refer to our children, our future? We talked freely of a generation that had fallen behind, who needed to catch up, a generation that would earn less, a generation of problems and suffering. We used a shaming language, a language of closed doors and of no hope. We needed to do better.

In 1968, Rosenthal and Jacobson wrote a seminal piece on how the expectations of teachers affect pupil performance. Simply put, when we expect others to behave in particular ways, we create a script that makes the behaviour more likely to occur. A teacher who believes that a pupil is high performing, expects higher performance and ultimately creates actual higher performance.

In 20 years of working in schools, I have seen how high expectations and positivity win every time and undoubtedly unlock potential. It saddened me to think that our negative talk of a lost *'Covid Generation'* – a disease generation – served only to perpetuate negativity and a self-fulfilling prophecy of no hope and failure. New leaders must set positive narratives.

Even if we don't learn the lesson from Rosenthal and Jacobson, we could look to brain science for more justification to change the narrative. Brain science shows us time and time again that negativity impinges on our brain performance. Emotionally charged negative thoughts divert energy from the pre-frontal cortex, used for cognitive function, to the limbic system (freeze, fight or flight) so you simply can't think as clearly. Negativity triggers stress hormones, making neuron activity less efficient. We must not label a generation negatively if we want them to think clearly, for all our futures.

I feel strongly that leaders have a moral obligation to our children to always shift the equilibrium to a positive narrative. In this case, a narrative that recognises that this generation have gone through something truly remarkable and where some may well indeed need support. This generation will rebuild, and they will create a more open and better society. This generation will be more resilient, they will value and seize what they have lost and they will go on to be remarkable.

I am optimistic about this generation and I want to dedicate our collective efforts as educators to helping these children who have experienced the remarkable, become remarkable. They were never the disease *'Covid Generation'*. They are The Remarkables. Let's forget the *'Covid Generation'* and focus on The Remarkables.

> *Leaders avoid negative narratives. Set high expectations through positive language. Unlock potential.*

REFLECTION QUESTION

Do leaders have a moral obligation to create a positive narrative? Why is this important?

TASKS

1. Think of the negative labels that you hear in your daily work. What impact do negative labels have? Are they self-fulfilling?
2. What steps can you take to challenge this and set a positive narrative?
3. How do you help create a remarkable generation?

Chapter 40
QUIET AMBITION

Ambition always reveals itself. And I am learning to spot it when it does because ambition fuels high performance.

Spending time with my friend David, a successful business owner, often gives me insight into a different way of thinking. He challenges me and reminds me that swagger, frankness and demanding thinking from others have their place. Our topic of discussion today was interviews and recruiting the right people. The intensity of the focused social interaction of an interview often reveals something interesting about human behaviour.

David's challenge was, *'Do you ever ask teachers to teach you something when you interview them?'* 'Well, we ask them to teach a lesson and watch,' I explain. *'No, no, no, that's not what I mean. Do you ever ask them to teach you something at an interview?'* 'Er ... no, suppose I don't,' I said.

It was Friday afternoon, and we were interviewing two teachers. As I listened, I thought of David and decided that, as headteacher, it was perfectly acceptable to ask a teacher to teach me something. I picked my moment and asked, *'Please would you teach me something?'*

As they and I stepped into the unknown, there appeared to be two very different behavioural reactions. First, *surprise*. *'What do you mean?'* I clarified by saying, *'You are a teacher, and I am looking for a teacher. Please teach me something.'* There followed *denial*, where they powerfully described how effective they thought they were in the classroom. The alternative reaction from the next candidate, engaged me – *a pause and launch into a different mode*. This colleague bounced into the role of teacher, gripped me with the subject, checked I understood, smiled, gave me confidence and encouraged me when I felt confused. This was better by far.

This experience made me reflect on how words, powerfully spoken, disguise performance and convince you artificially that someone is better than they truly are. We listen carefully to the words spoken at interviews and put such faith in them. The unfounded claims of those who speak with excessive confidence can easily influence our thinking.

When I think of the most successful and high-performing colleagues around me, they are the ones that *pause and launch* in their work. When they complete their work and when they have performed at the highest level, they are bashful and modest. When you compliment them, they look away and say, '*it was nothing, I was just doing my job*'. They play the good game, rather than talking a good game.

These individuals behave with quiet ambition. An ambition that feels like it has turned in on itself, rather than out through exaggerated confidence. They display ambition by simply being the very best version of themselves through their actions. When I ask these colleagues what they would like to achieve next in their career, they say '*I'm not sure*'. They want to be the best that they can be, *presently*. These are the colleagues who progress and deliver again, then progress and deliver again.

We appointed the teacher who *paused and launched*, and they went on to win the respect of our pupils and delivered exciting new initiatives. When I think about colleagues with quiet ambition, they reveal a purpose in their everyday behaviour to give their best. They achieve this with their actions and not just confident words. In doing so, they make a difference and progress in their careers. New leaders would be wise to see beyond the empty words of those who talk about being ambitious and look for those who are quietly ambitious. Those who pause and launch.

Watch out for unfounded claims and excessively confident voices that sway your thinking easily. Look for quiet ambition.

REFLECTION QUESTION

Why have you been duped by words, powerfully spoken, that disguise performance and convince you artificially that someone is better than they truly are?

TASKS

1. What is quiet ambition?
2. Can you identify who has it in your team?
3. How do you check unfounded claims and excessively confident voices?

Chapter 41

THE MISCONCEPTION OF STRONG LEADERSHIP

I dislike reductionistic conceptions of leadership, particularly the *'strong leader'*. I have never heard of a patient asking to see the *'strong doctor'* or the *'strong nurse'*. I can't imagine the fire service agreeing to send the *'strong firefighter'*. It amuses me to think that I might be a *'medium strength'* leader who, with training, could become a *'strong leader'*. This is a crass way of thinking, and I dislike the toxic notions of masculinity and the patriarchal assumptions of the *'strong'* leader.

I remember being taught by a PhD student at university. With his can of Coke in front of him and his watch placed on the desk to keep a track of time, he ripped through the history of political philosophy whilst giving simple examples to help us understand. I remember him explaining *'abstraction'*. He pointed to his jacket and asked me to abstract something out of his jacket to understand *'jacket-ness'*. I was stuck, so he told me to *'pick a feature, imagine lifting that feature out of the jacket and the feature is then hovering above the jacket'*. I spot the jacket is black and made of leather and say, *'black leather'*. He smiles and says, *'one feature'*, so I respond with *'leather'*.

'OK, we have now abstracted "leather-ness" out of the jacket, so here we have the problem with abstraction. Looking now at "leather-ness", hovering in the air, without the jacket, does it tell you anything about jacket-ness?' Absolutely not.

The abstraction is obscure and useless; just like *'strong leadership'*. Imagine now a room filled with football players. You ask them to go to the front of the room if they are a *'strong footballer'* and the back of the room if they are a *'weak footballer'*. You then ask them to go to the right-hand side of the room if they are an *'outstanding footballer'* or the left-hand side if they are a *'good footballer'*.

This is the thinking when we talk about *'strong leadership'*; it is a waste of time. Reducing leadership down to banal categories makes leadership appear simple. I have learnt that leadership is far more complex and better understood across different continuums.

A different way of thinking about this is to re-imagine all the football players in the room. But this time ten lines are drawn across the room. You ask the footballers to all stand on the first line – the line of effective defending – and ask them to order themselves from high to low. You ask them to go to the next line – the line of effective shooting. And then the next – the line of effective passing. And so on. In this line of thinking, we see a much more sophisticated view of the footballing individual across a range of lines of effectiveness. We build a much more detailed understanding of their footballing profile. This model has placed performance across different continuums.

When I hear the phrase *'strong leadership'*, I think of the two very different rooms. I ask myself to smash the reductionism and think about continuums. What are the ten lines of effective leadership and where do I fit on each of those lines? Which ones do I need to work on and which ones take precedence in different situations? What are your lines of effective leadership as a new leader?

My ten continuums are:

1. positivity;
2. humility;
3. visibility;
4. working with others;
5. listening;
6. setting direction;
7. confidence;
8. clarity;
9. creativity;
10. organisation.

My list may change as I develop. But, whilst I dislike reductionism, I can simplify my list of ten to two or three that are the most important aspects of my leadership. It is never just *'strong leadership'*. That is a worthless abstraction.

New leaders should think about leadership along lines of effectiveness where you don't have to be on the right-hand side, or score highly for every line, to be an effective leader. Be clear on your lines, focusing your development on the areas where you have room for improvement.

> *Avoid seeing leadership in simplistic terms of the* 'strong leader'. *Break it down into key themes and focus on developing in each area.*

REFLECTION QUESTION

Why is it problematic to reduce leadership to being a *'strong leader'*?

TASKS

1. What are your ten lines of effective leadership?
2. For each line score yourself 1–10, 10 being highly effective in this area. Which theme do you need to focus on?
3. Would others agree with your scores?
4. Reduce your ten lines to three main continuums that are the most important for you.

Chapter 42
BENCHES

All friends have a bench story. David and I sat on a bench in the port car park in Palma, Mallorca. We admired his achievement, a finely parked car in the tightest of bays. However, our two 15 year-old sons sat in the back of the car, heads bowed, looking at their phones, having had enough of the heat, now refusing to join us for an evening meal. We discussed how and who was going to break the news to our wives that we had failed to get the boys out of the car. We explored various options, all increasingly ridiculous, as we laughed about how plans to rest and relax on holiday sometimes go awry.

Then, a car arrived – a large green people carrier – and attempted to park in the next very tight bay. We took notice, after the fifth attempt to park, when a passenger jumped out to assist the struggling driver. At the tenth attempt, we had easily forgotten about our grumpy 15 year-olds, distracted by the parking crisis unfolding in front of our bench. The passenger became animated in their support of the struggling driver, shouting *'einschlag, einschlag'*. Engrossed and with scant regard for the imploding embarrassment of the driver, I felt it appropriate to intervene and give my support. Instead of *'einschlag'*, I elected to urge the driver to *'back, back, back, now swing, swing'*. The driver heard a mixture of *'einschlag, back, back, einschlag, back, back, swing'*. Helpful, I'm sure.

Now, even more distracted from our *leaving-the-car-refusing-15 year-olds*, I became curious to understand the meaning of *'einschlag'*. Our wives returned to see their ageing husbands, worn by the heat of the day, sitting on a bench shouting *'was ist einschlag?'* across the car park to the driver. Subsequently, they ejected the boys from the car, and ejected us from the comfort of our bench, to follow them and the boys, now compliant, for our meal.

David and I often refer to our *einschlag* story and this binds our friendship, a textured layer of experience, based on a tiny incident in a car park. It was a shared experience that only friends would fully understand. I think all friends have a bench story and that gives solidarity to their companionship.

My mum has a different way of understanding the importance of benches in human relationships. Her view is that benches are important because it is *'where futures are discussed'*. I like the idea of benches being a place of focus where we talk about our hopes and dreams. She has a 1960s black-and-white photo of her oldest friendship where they first discussed boys they liked and getting married.

We have memorial benches in school. I find it poignant when pupils return and sit on the bench dedicated to the loss of a close friend. It moves me to see flowers resting at the leg of the bench. These benches connect us to memories of those we have lost.

As new leaders establish themselves in their school's community and realise that relationships and trust take time, think about whether you have a bench story for every one of your colleagues. This can be hard in a large organisation, but something to strive for. New leaders need to commit to bench stories.

Strive to find a connection with every member of staff.

REFLECTION QUESTION

Do you have a bench story for every one of your colleagues?

TASKS

1. Identify colleagues in your school that you don't know well and don't feel connected with.
2. Ask questions, share experiences, take part and say yes to activities that give the opportunity to find a bench story.
3. Are you curious and interested enough in the lives of people who serve the community you lead? Do they know you are interested?

Chapter 43
THE SELF-EMPLOYED MINDSET

I worked with a colleague whose desk was always clear – his to-do list completed every day and nothing in his email account. Even in the most challenging of times, on the busiest of days, he would tick the tasks off, and his desk would remain clear.

Clinically organised, efficient and motivated by tasks, work was getting done. For someone who has a life of endlessly flagged emails, constantly rewritten lists, almost always longer than the previous day, scribbled on late into the night as the residue of the day passes through my mind, I found this way of working difficult to comprehend. Told off for glancing at my email or replying to a work message when I'd just walked through the door of my home, why could I not be one of those task-ticker types?

Not as a test, but merely to understand, I asked him to walk with me and show me where we were with things in his area of responsibility. As we talked and as I tried to understand, I heard time and time again him using the phrase *'I've done that'*, *'I did that'*, and then *'I asked someone to do that'*. Increasingly frustrated and annoyed, I said, *'I know you have done this; you have told me. I know you have asked someone to do this or that, but has it happened, and has it worked?'* Frustrated, he replied, *'I don't know. But, I have asked. ... Definitely, I've asked them'*.

Colleagues like this write action plans and then write the same action plan a month or year later. They forward emails for others to reply, they leave instructions to do work on the voicemails of others and tick off the task on their list. These colleagues conjure a smokescreen of efficiency, a rabbit out of the hat.

Task-ticker types no longer convince me. At first, I thought, they must be good leaders as they get things done. But the issue is simple. In the race to finish the job, they forget to *inspect what they expect*. They fail to check in with people to see what progress they have made. They fail to show an interest in others as they are only interested in their task-ticking. They fail to challenge others, so long as they have ticked the task. They fail to evaluate, and their leadership may have the impact of a misfired rubber band hitting the wall and flopping to the floor.

This task-ticker type of leader lives a working life where they never put the burglar alarm on because other people do this for them. The leader who checks the alarm before going home is a different type of leader, one who adopts a *self-employed mindset*. They don't just send an email, they follow up and know that impact matters. This is because they take responsibility. When the lights need to be off, they check them. They care. They approach work as if it were their own business, a business they started or a family business with years of tradition that they are proud to be a part of. They don't forget that they have left the important files in their top drawer. They always know where the important files are because it is their business to know. It doesn't matter if the email comes in late and fires a need to act. They take responsibility and take action.

One of the most successful leaders that I worked for told me that '*you are the headteacher of your area*'. I heard him say this to others and understand now the expectation that he was setting – a headteacher takes responsibility and if you look after your area like I do the school, everything will work fine. He was asking others to take responsibility, turn the lights off and know how to set their own burglar alarm.

I have learnt that whilst there is a place for task-ticking, the very best leaders adopt a very different approach. They have a *self-employed mindset* in all they do. Their impact on others and the pride they have in their work matter more than task-ticking so they can arrive home early. This type of leader picks rubbish off the floor, straightens the picture and grapples hard with the larger items. Then, they set their own burglar alarm. Look out for those with a *self-employed mindset*. They are leaders.

Leaders take responsibility and adopt a self-employed mindset.

REFLECTION QUESTION

Do the very best leaders adopt a *self-employed mindset*?

TASKS

1. List the three most effective leaders that you have worked for.
2. What role does responsibility play in their effective leadership?
3. How do others perceive your leadership? Do you display a *self-employed mindset*?

Chapter 44

TAKING MEASURED RISKS

When you think about the meaning of risk – exposure to harm, danger or loss – you feel you have just opened your eyes to look at your feet on a glass floor, at the very top of a skyscraper.

The journey to Birmingham from Leeds for the annual Association of School Leaders conference is a time of excitement. Stepping out of the school to join nearly a thousand school leaders listening to ideas about the future of education, you can't help but look forward to this event. Kirstie and I were travelling together on Thursday evening and our conversation was about whether we should take a risk.

During the day, we had been interviewing for a new faculty leader. We faced a decision between someone who had done the job before, who had experience, and someone who had only three years of teaching experience, who had brilliant ideas and who was an exceptional individual. Do you take the risk or not?

I have learnt that new leaders should seize the opportunity to take risks. Because if they are successful decisions, then measured risk-taking can have a tenfold impact. Whilst the risk and the consequences ultimately sit with you, if you are comfortable that you have been measured in your risk-taking, then it is time for you to take a risk.

Often, the recruitment of staff involves risk. I have faced various situations where the process has resulted in a choice between a *safe option* and *risk option*. But how do you know whether you should take the risky route?

Changing well-established routines also closely links with risk. You really need to shatter the existing practice but feel the exposure of it going badly wrong. Given the potential impact of taking such a risk, it is not surprising that new leaders need to consider their own relationship with risk.

We seem conditioned to fear risk in how we approach hazards at work. We plan to mitigate them by completing risk registers and risk assessments. This type of thinking points you towards risk aversion and makes it difficult to see risk-taking as a positive in leading well. But what can help new leaders to take risks? I have learnt three strategies which I call *the risk prerequisites for the risk averse*. Fulfilling each of the prerequisites helps me to take risks.

Take the risk when the safer option is much worse than the risk option failing. Faced with a risky decision, it is likely that you are working in an area that needs to change. Think carefully about where the *safe option* would take you versus the *risk option* failing. In the worst scenario, if the *risk option* failing is better than the *safe option*, then you have fulfilled the prerequisite. Take the risk. If you have taken a measured risk, there will probably be a tenfold impact, anyway.

Take the risk so long as you haven't decided entirely alone. You need help when you make risky decisions. On the train to Birmingham, Kirstie and I had been working through whether the safer option was worse than the risky option failing. Talking this through with colleagues you trust and who stress-test your thinking helps you to do this effectively. Critical debate takes you out of your *Kopfkino* and gives you the strength to take the risk.

Take the risk knowing that there is always another solution or way out if you must change direction. This final prerequisite needs to be thought through, as it is often the last nudge that allows you to step out and take the risk. Take confidence that you have the resources and expertise to have another go to make things better if this decision doesn't work.

I decided on the train to Birmingham to go for the inexperienced but exceptional individual for our new faculty. I had checked that I had fulfilled the prerequisites, and I needed to move things forward. He went on to effect impressive change.

Even when you fulfil the prerequisites, you can never entirely see the unintended consequence of the decisions you make. Big changes indeed create riptides. Learn to embrace the risky intended consequence but see the riptides of unintended effects as an opportunity for further development and areas of focus.

The most effective risk-taking, however, takes place with the *self-employed mindset* where you approach your work as if it were your own family business – a business you are the custodian of for the next generation. The *self-employed mindset* is then an effective counterbalance to the risk. Take risk-taking seriously and trust that it will take your school forward.

> *Seize the opportunity to take risks when the safe option is worse than the risk option failing.*

REFLECTION QUESTION

What is your attitude to risk as a new school leader?

TASKS

1. Think of some examples where you made safe and risky decisions.
2. For each example, analyse them in terms of the three strategies – *the risk prerequisites for the risk averse*. Was your decision the most effective?
3. What steps can you take so that you reason through your own risk-taking?

Chapter 45

THE PITFALL OF THE SELF-EMPLOYED MINDSET

Setting the burglar alarm at school makes me feel nervous. A sinking feeling when the beeps time you out of the building. The site manager taught me to turn the alarm on and off. He sets the alarm so effortlessly, the years of experience normalising what makes me take an extra breath. The first time I had to do this there was no time for overthinking. I just needed to turn it off so we could crack on.

It had been a week of responding to government guidance, planning, meetings and re-planning. I had spent much of the week online, in school, but school wasn't feeling like it should. A tiny number of children of key workers were attending, the rest of the school population at home, whilst everything was being reworked – from remote lessons, vouchers for free school meals, recruitment for the following year, to simply trying to keep everything going.

My two colleagues who with me form a leadership trio would say *'yes'*. They always do. At the very early stage of the pandemic, the design teachers had gone the extra mile and worked out how to make PPE visors that we were distributing to local care homes, dentists, doctors' surgeries and hospitals. It was a remarkable achievement and gave the team meaning in such a period of uncertainty. I remember saying to Kirstie, '*I need to do something practical after being in online meetings all week. Do you want to make some masks on Saturday?*' '*Of course, yes*', she said. What else was there to do during a lockdown weekend than for us to come into school?

Kirstie with her daughter, Tim with his daughter, and my wife and I, arrived in school on Saturday morning to manufacture 300 visors – even if that meant turning the burglar alarm off.

Why do some leaders always say *'yes'*? Whatever their workload and however busy they are, if someone asks for their help, they say *'yes'*. They live out the *self-employed mindset*. Their days get busier and busier with their own work often being pushed into moments later in the day. They selflessly give to others, often at the expense of their own time. The impact on their personal lives can be significant; they just don't have the time for themselves.

We say *'yes'* for many reasons, believing that leaders should give selflessly to others. We say *'yes'* because we often know the answer and how to solve the problem. We fall into the trap of thinking it is quicker and easier to solve the problem ourselves, so we just say *'yes'* and take on the work. We say *'yes'* because we want to please others. We sometimes say *'yes'* and flit to the next task as the task at hand is difficult, and the interruption is actually a timely distraction. We say *'yes'* because we don't want to miss the opportunity. When we say *'yes, yes, yes'* our days fill up. But we take on workloads that would make a superhero wince. Often, we say *'yes'* because we find it hard to say *'no'*.

The pitfall of the *self-employed mindset* is that we forget how to say *'no'*. We would be wise to remind ourselves of why saying *'no'* benefits others and strengthens our leadership. By saying *'no'*, we take control of our own plans for how we are going to spend our time. We achieve the things that we set out to do in the time that we allocated to the task. Some tasks just need to be done and space needs to be created for their completion. Saying *'no'* marks boundaries, sets expectations and displays clarity of thinking. By saying *'no'*, we mark a line, a boundary that

The Pitfall of the Self-Employed Mindset

clarifies to others what should happen. By saying 'no' to diving in with the answer, we help others to find their own solution to the issue. We foster self-responsibility and personal development.

Knowing when to say 'no' is an important part of leading. New leaders would be wise to train themselves to be entirely comfortable about saying 'no'. Avoid the pitfalls of the *self-employed mindset*, with a very simple two-letter word and one-word sentence. No.

> *Judging when to say 'no' encourages others to take responsibility and creates time.*

REFLECTION QUESTION

When should leaders say, 'yes' and when should they say 'no'?

TASKS

1. What is the pitfall of the *self-employed mindset*?
2. Why, especially, do new leaders often say 'yes'?
3. Practise saying 'no'.

Chapter 46

THREADS

When I worked as a deputy headteacher, I spoke with my headteacher about how we could improve *'scholarliness'* in our sixth form. If all pupils adopted the *'scholarly'* habits of the highest performing pupils, then we should see increased performance. We laughed about the word *'scholarliness'* as neither of us could really say the word. I was training to be a headteacher, studying the National Professional Qualification for Headship at the time, and decided to develop scholarliness into the concept of *academic productivity*. Pupils could have higher or lower *academic productivity*, depending on how much time they spent on tasks and how they used their time when studying. By studying the habits of the highest performing pupils, the time they spent and the tasks that they performed, we could begin to understand their *academic productivity*.

I gradually introduced this term to staff, not a flawless concept by any means, but something that took hold – a thread. Over time, we carried out research with pupils, parents and staff. We identified high-return tasks that boosted productivity. We rewarded pupils for high academic productivity and even built a measure of productivity into the reports to parents. When I heard the term being used by others, I thought about the responsibility we have as leaders to sew the right *thread*.

I would like the values, goals and initiatives of our school to be at the fingertips of all colleagues – a shared set of ideas that we all collectively strive to achieve. A visitor should be able to talk with any member of staff and they should hear the same goals and ideas being explained. I hope visitors would describe us as *'sharp'* and *'tight'*.

Durkheim, one of the founders of sociology, described how societies have a tendency towards stability and order. But he used the concept of *anomie* to explain disruption and periods of normlessness (Giddens, 1972). Despite the uncertainty of large-scale changes such as a pandemic or recession that cause anomie, societies return to order, solidarity and collective conscience. I aim for our collective conscience and our solidarity to be understood and shared by all.

This aim is important because, although it is difficult to measure, it is the tangible impact of a leader. If my senior team and I are effective, the organisation and culture should be *'together'*, our values, goals and initiatives tightly woven, creating a collective bond of positive focus. New leaders should think much more clearly in terms of threads. If we select the right threads and routinely revisit them, the initiative will take hold.

Make sure that the initial thread is simple, based on evidence and on what is possible. It should be easy to say, easy to understand, memorable and applicable across all teams in the school. The best threads are not only aspirational and straightforward to understand at an organisational level, but also actionable for an individual.

I have seen several threads – *making learning stick, silent time, academic productivity, instructional coaching, explicit vocabulary instruction* and *meeting need*. All of them are great threads and make a difference – some stay and others fade away. But my new thread seems to take me back to why I became a teacher. I like the thread of *zero gaps*, which tackles the hand served to the most disadvantaged children by redoubling our efforts and opportunities so they achieve at the rate that they truly should. Not *'close the gap'*, this has lower aspiration baked in, but *zero gaps*.

I am learning to think more clearly about threads – so much so that I write '*A4-0-gaps*' on the top of my notebook every day: *aim for zero-gaps*. Unashamedly talk about your threads, relentlessly creating a shared understanding. If you keep stitching the thread in the hardest-to-reach area, a seam will form. And if you stitch this well together, the gap will become seamless. You will have a seamless culture of well-thought-out and well-implemented threads.

> *Forge action through simple threads, based on evidence and aspiration. Then, talk about them relentlessly.*

REFLECTION QUESTION

What are the most effective leadership '*threads*'? Why are they important?

TASKS

1. Identify the key leadership '*threads*' that you have implemented.
2. Which one was the most effective in terms of simplicity, evidence to support and aspiration for children?
3. Focus on a thread that you can talk about unashamedly, relentlessly creating a shared understanding.

Chapter 47
TUNING FORKS

Colleague 1 arrived for an interview for an internal leadership position. A member of my senior team, said earlier in the day, *'look out for Colleague 1. They look sharp today'*. Colleague 1 looked the part, wearing a very smart suit.

Colleague 2, going for the same job, dressed as he always dressed. His answers found a rhythm and when asked to speak openly about how he would move things forward, he gave an honest and well-intentioned answer about what he would do.

If you never wear a suit but turn up for an internal interview wearing one, something doesn't feel quite right. If you give a well-intentioned answer about something you would do, but you have been saying the same thing in your current role, and have never delivered it, you have a problem. Both colleagues 1 and 2 had hurdles to overcome. For one, a hurdle of consistency. For the other, a hurdle of delivery. Difficult jumps to make when you haven't made the jump before.

We can't escape the fact that when we take on new leadership roles, people notice things about us. The way we hold ourselves when we walk into a room, the consistency of our mood and the way we dress. I remember buying a smartwatch so that I could be more efficient – a calendar pinging on my wrist. I wore the watch to work and delivered a briefing online. Later in the day, meeting with a colleague, they said, *'I noticed you had a new watch'*. They had only noticed the watch.

I had to work from home when I tested positive for Covid-19. I woke that morning and put on my shirt and tie, made a coffee and prepared to deliver a similar briefing. A few weeks later, I talked with a colleague. She asked me if I had recovered from Covid-19 and said, '*I noticed when you were at home you still wore a tie*'.

A visitor to our school once said, '*little things matter here*'. He was talking about how we fly diversity flags and how we wear rainbow colours on our lanyards. Little things do matter, and if leaders take their ties off, so will others. If leaders arrive late, so will others. We often think that standards come from enforcing the rules, but standards come from somewhere else. Standards start with the leader – from what you say, what you don't say and what others see. Leaders have an inevitable influence on others because of the privileged position they hold. They act like tuning forks in every interaction that they hold.

Sometimes they get this wrong. I had to speak with a member of my senior team for regularly being late. He arrived just after meetings started, adopting a very purposeful stride into the room that said, '*I am efficient, and I am busy. In fact, it's amazing that I am here at all*'. No. They had struck the wrong tuning fork. Unfortunately, he was out of tune. He was simply late.

He needed to understand that he was a tuning fork for lateness. That needed to be stopped. Leaders need to have a collection of correct tuning forks. They also need to remember that they may well be a tuning fork for less desirable behaviour. Therefore, they need to be prepared to look at themselves. I remember a headteacher telling me I needed a haircut and a new pair of shoes. I'd picked up the wrong fork.

Colleagues 1 and 2 weren't successful. I gave them feedback and they learnt an important lesson about consistent standards and delivering on what you say you are going to deliver – a lesson about tuning forks. As a new leader, set the standard. Your behaviour matters.

Leaders are noticed; set the standard you want others to see and be.

REFLECTION QUESTION

What standard do you set?

TASKS

1. Take an honest look at the standard you set in how you present as a leader. What impression are you giving in what you say and don't say?
2. Think carefully about other leaders around you in terms of *'tuning forks'*. What standards are they setting for others?
3. Take action to address your own *'tuning forks'* and those of others through effective feedback.

Chapter 48

PIPELINES

I remember seeing the Pompidou Centre for the first time. Jasmin, my not-yet adopted daughter, was eight years old. We were visiting Paris for the first time. Wearing her *best-bright-white-linen-dress*, we walked, one hand in mine and the other firmly rooted in the loving hand of Mum. The night before, I'd explained that tomorrow we were going to see a special building. *'Really,'* she said, *'the insides of the building are on the outside?'* After a long pause, I replied, *'yes, really, the pipes and lifts and everything, the insides on the outside'*. *'Oh'*, Jasmin replied, with a questioning look.

I think leaders would react like Jasmin, with a ponderous *'oh'*, if they could see the *'insides on the outside'* of their school. My view is that the very best organisations have the most impressive pipework; lots and lots of pipework, different shapes, different materials, some old, some new, beautiful pipework. Pipes, pipework and pipelines transport the essential ingredients that make organisations great.

In schools, pipelines that deliver the very best teachers make the job of a headteacher so much easier. We have a fabulous pipeline of trainee teachers who successfully secure teaching jobs with us. We have another pipeline that allows talented individuals to access a range of middle leadership and then senior leadership positions. We have a pipeline feeding in from leadership qualifications that are available to staff. We have pipelines that feed out, where talented staff move to other schools. There is another pipeline that returns them to school, to more senior positions, when they have gained further experience.

That said, I think sometimes the pipelines become a little disorganised – old pipes and new pipes, not always connecting as well as they should. Teachers who almost join us, skilled teachers who have missed the pipe and teachers who may have gone down the wrong pipe. New leaders should think more deeply about pipelines. You need multiple pipelines that bring the best staff in, multiple pipelines that allow staff to move forward and pipelines that deliver the next generation.

I look at two of my closest colleagues and the leadership trio that we form. I have fallen into a misguided trap that this trio has permanence. I rely on them and can't imagine not leading with them. The thought of them moving elsewhere makes me think of closing doors, rather than opening pipes. But this leadership trio needs a pipeline too, in and out, if our school is to remain successful. Leaders can't stay forever. Not least because, if they do, the pipes just get blocked. Leaders grow wings, and the time comes for them to fly. I need to think about a pipeline for my role as headteacher. What do I want to do next and which pipes do I want to consider? Leaders can't sit still.

Pipelines need to be treated with respect because things become very messy if they burst. I have a colleague who is an exceptional teacher. She has served the school for the best part of 40 years, and she looks after our trainee teachers. We try to have a trainee in each department, a crucial pipeline. Given the importance of pipelines, it is only right that you entrust the pipeline to the right person. This colleague will feed us the best teachers based on her knowledge of our culture and her ability to see potential. Three of her most recent recommendations have just taken up leadership positions after less than five years of experience. This colleague has a superpower, looking after a pipeline that takes our school effectively into the future. A pipeline that connects the immediate past to the future.

I work with another colleague who has a similar superpower of pipeline control. She sits to the right of me in interview panels and we know each other's questions, the way we phrase them and the meaning we are trying to elicit. She watches the interviewee and listens carefully to their answers. She sits back and processes all the evidence we have gathered during the day. When we finish all the interviews, I ask her to speak first. I know and trust that she will open the valve to the pipeline for the right person.

I am thinking more and more about the future of the school in terms of the next generation. Who are the leaders that will lead next? Leaders need to build effective pipelines, reasonably organised and diverse pipelines, pipelines that connect outside and inside, and pipelines that connect to the different roles in the school. Pipelines are networks that leaders must build every day through the connections we have and the opportunities we give to others. New leaders would be wise to embrace conversations about someone new emerging from the pipeline. These conversations are about opportunity and building the future. Like Jasmin hearing about the Pompidou Centre, with a ponderous glance ... *'Really, oh yes, they will be brilliant in that role.'*

> *Ensure you have a range of effective staffing pipelines into, through and out of your school.*

REFLECTION **QUESTION**

What pipelines exist, at all levels, into, through and out of your school?

TASKS

1. Carry out an in-depth analysis for each team in your school. Who are the emerging leaders and what opportunities do they have to develop?
2. Are all the pipelines working effectively? Where are the blockages?
3. What steps can you take to ensure the pipelines are functioning effectively?

Chapter 49

WORKING SIDEWAYS ACROSS SCHOOLS

> *The secret to a world-class education is a mixture of some top-down, some bottom-up and, most importantly, a great deal of lateral development and sharing of effective practice between teachers, leaders, schools and local authorities. The difference good leadership can make should never be underestimated, and if we get this sharing and distribution of expertise right it can really make a difference to the whole system.*
>
> (Munby, 2019, p 94)

My coach smiled knowingly when she saw my reaction to my personal-drivers report based on the Odin Development Compass. ODC is a development tool designed to understand behaviours that give you energy and those that drain you as a leader. It helps reveal your natural leadership preferences, your unconscious drivers and your competence in certain areas. It reveals natural strengths, unlocked potential and fragile strengths.

'How can I be an effective headteacher, if I have a fragile strength of leading?' I asked in exasperation.

My coach knew she needed to explain things calmly and precisely.

> *Fragile strengths are areas that you have learnt to be good at and others see you as competent in these areas. But if you are tired and facing extreme pressure, a set of negative behaviours are likely to emerge. These could be negative*

behaviours like becoming dominant, authoritarian, and overly assertive.

The Odin method and my coach forced me to think about my fragile strength and areas for development. I talked them through with my wife, children and with Kirstie at work. Kirstie is an exceptional professional whom I have worked with for a good length of time. She has been my co-pilot running the school and always gives me an honest and challenging perspective. I remember taking a Myers-Briggs test alongside her at a leadership weekend and we laughed as my results contained the exact opposite to hers. I knew she would have a handle on my fragile strength. Kirstie reminded me to not be too critical of myself.

I was shocked, though, to think that leading was a fragile strength. Something that I have learnt to do, worked hard to do, but something that ultimately drains me and costs me energy.

My coach knew it was time to move me along and encouraged me to think about my natural strengths and areas of natural potential. Areas of natural potential are *'goldmine'* areas for development. Areas that are straightforward for you, energising and enjoyable – areas that once realised become natural strengths. You can do them all day and they don't sap your energy in any way.

Struck by this way of thinking, despite becoming gradually more comfortable and confident in my role, I needed to learn to manage my fragile strength, recognising when negative behaviours pop out. I needed to unlock natural potential in identified areas of collaboration, empathy and building relationships – *'goldmine'* opportunities for development.

These areas had been on my mind when thinking about my wider role as a leader within a Multi-Academy Trust (MAT). There are undoubtedly challenges of being a headteacher in a MAT. There are no doubt even greater and unique challenges of working in a single academy, local authority school or any other way a society organises schooling. MATs, however, have their own unique qualities and challenges.

MATs are new. They are a collection of schools that have their own unique history and culture, which may well be geographically distant from each other and may contain schools of different types, needs and different ages. New MATs feel like new families, families who don't know each other, but who have high expectations about getting along. New families take time to build relationships, take time to get to know each other and take time to form bonds of trust.

The next challenge is complex. Trusts suffer from reification – where something that is abstract, a Trust, is represented as a concrete thing. A MAT may be made of 20 schools and 15,000 children; it is a collection of individuals and many processes. If you took away the schools, however, Trusts simply wouldn't exist. In contrast, you can't separate the school from its pupils as they are more concrete, with distinct cultures, values and history. The risk of reification pops out in phrases like *'the Trust has asked us to do this'*, *'ask the Trust'* or *'what does the Trust want?'* MATs are a collection of people and not an entity in themselves.

Schools in MATs may collaborate easily with each other, share ideas and work together for the benefit of all. But the ultimate barrier to achieving this is about how leaders within each school engage with each other. This, combined with overcoming the frustration of reification and the challenge of building relationships within such new organisations is the next step in my learning to lead.

With my coach, I focused on how my own areas of potential can overcome these challenges. If I show empathy, I can understand how difficult it must be for a CEO to lead a group of headteachers – thinking of all those fragile strengths playing themselves out in meetings.

I can understand that my decision-making for the school could be at odds with the decision-making for all schools. Empathy tells me it is hard for a MAT to create a culture and shared purpose from a collection of different unique cultures. By understanding this, I am better placed to help and shape the overall culture. By developing my empathy, I understand that the new relationships between the schools and people within them need to be built through positivity and generosity to each other.

Although sideways working has a long history at the school where I work, training teachers and leaders from other schools, working in groups with other schools and simply helping others, you can always do more. I have started to use the phrase *sideways working* in my leadership, talking about it and modelling it. I want others to see this as expected behaviour. It is important that we identify how we share resources, and create opportunities for work shadowing, visits and collaborative meetings for all.

My last lesson in leadership is a goldmine. Understanding your fragile strengths, and understanding that others have their own fragile strengths, allows you to better understand yourself and others, especially when working sideways. Leaders are in no way perfect or ever the finished article. It intrigues me to think that unlocked potential, understanding fragile strengths, and those of other leaders, have a role to play in the development of schools.

Steve Munby (2019) wrote that the secret of a world-class education is *'most importantly [a] great deal of lateral development'*. I have learnt that I can have an impact far beyond the school that I lead if, when I work sideways, I start from the position of *'how can I help to make a difference beyond my school and how can I work with you to make this happen?'* This has to be the locked-in mindset and the future of working in MATs and all schools across the land. A future for new leaders that is worth fighting for, with empathy, of course.

> *When you work sideways across schools, start from the position of how you can help to make a difference. How can you work with others to make this happen?*

REFLECTION QUESTION

How can you help to make a difference beyond your school for the benefit of children and the future lives of children that don't yet exist?

Part 4
SUMMARY

Leading every day requires a commitment to having the right mindset and setting the right culture. New leaders should set ambitious goals and stick to them. Goals prevent distraction, give meaning and create that space, just in front of you, where success can flourish. Being driven towards goals is only possible when you have a positive and respectful culture. This can be fostered as a new leader by embracing praise to kindle the emotion of pride. This motivates others through effective recognition.

Positive cultures are also built through listening, adapting, communicating solutions and acting with compassion. New leaders should avoid negative narratives and set high expectations through positive language.

Being enthusiastic and curious is important as a new leader, but watch out for unfounded claims and excessively confident voices that sway your thinking easily. Look for colleagues to support you that work with *'quiet ambition'*. These are leaders who don't see themselves as simply *'strong leaders'* but have a range of leadership qualities.

Building a positive culture is ultimately about people and relationships. Strive to find a connection with every member of staff. Another way of doing this is by showing that you care about the organisation – pick up rubbish, turn the lights off and grapple to find solutions. New leaders must take responsibility and adopt a *self-employed mindset*. The *self-employed mindset* also plays a role in taking risks. It is an effective counterbalance when making challenging risks. However, seize the opportunity to take risks when the safe option is worse than the risk option failing. Also remember, with the *self-employed mindset*, not to overdo things by judging when to say *'no'*. This encourages others to take responsibility and creates time for you to lead.

Cultures need concepts to frame action and set the direction. New leaders would be wise to forge action through simple ideas or threads, based on evidence and aspiration. They must then talk relentlessly about them. Concepts and goals alone are not enough. Remember that leaders are noticed. How you behave matters, so set the standard you want others to see and be. Rob Higgins, headteacher of The Blue Coat School, stresses this point with his advice on leading culture – be clear on the collective purpose and sweat the small stuff.

Schools develop and change all the time. New leaders need to be mindful of this and ensure they have a range of effective staffing pipelines into, through and out of their organisation. This protects the long-term future of your school. Finally, when working sideways across schools, start from the position of how you can help to make a difference. How you can work with others to bring about a better future.

Part 4 Case study

Rob Higgins on leading every day: mindset and culture

Leader	Rob Higgins
Setting	The Blue Coat School, Cranmer Education Trust, Oldham – secondary school of 1700 pupils
Role	Headteacher
If you could give two pieces of advice to a new school leader on	Be clear on the collective purpose. Systems and processes come and go but the core values of what everyone is working towards and why everyone chooses to work in the organisation remain constant. These are the values that help you get through the tough

| how to develop a positive culture, what would you say? | times and are also the foundations that shape celebrations and any positive news you have to share.

Sweat the small stuff – if it's important to you it's important. Don't assume everyone else will automatically notice or deliver your non-negotiables unless you are continually reinforcing, modelling and checking. |
|---|---|
| What is the most important leadership book to you? | Ferguson, A (1999) *Managing My Life: My Autobiography*. London: Hodder & Stoughton. |
| Why is this book important? | My guilty pleasures – football and Manchester United. Also, in this book there is so much about creating culture and how to get the best out of different people. |
| Give one piece of leadership advice to new school leaders. | Enjoy the role. Leadership is challenging at times but also a fabulous privilege. Make sure you build in the time to walk around school and talk to children and staff. It reminds you that all the hard work is worth it. |

Part 4 Key points

Leading every day: mindset and culture

1. Enjoy your relationship with ambitious goals; they prevent distraction, give meaning and create that space, just in front, where success can flourish.
2. Embrace praise to kindle the emotion of pride. This motivates others through effective recognition.

3. Listening, adapting, communicating solutions to concerns and acting with compassion fosters trust and even gratitude.
4. Leaders avoid negative narratives. Set high expectations through positive language. Unlock potential.
5. Watch out for unfounded claims and excessively confident voices that sway your thinking easily. Look for quiet ambition.
6. Avoid seeing leadership in simplistic terms of the *'strong leader'*. Break it down into themes and focus on developing in each area.
7. Strive to find a connection with every member of staff.
8. Leaders take responsibility and adopt a self-employed mindset.
9. Seize the opportunity to take risks when the safe option is worse than the risk-option failing.
10. Judging when to say *'no'* encourages others to take responsibility and creates time.
11. Forge action through simple threads, based on evidence and aspiration. Then, talk relentlessly about them.
12. Leaders are noticed; set the standard you want others to see and be.
13. Ensure you have a range of effective staffing pipelines into, through and out of your school.
14. When working sideways across schools, start from the position of how you can help to make a difference. How can you work with others to make this happen?

CONCLUSION

We all have stories that our families often tell. Sometimes the retelling of the story makes the memory. One of our stories is a tale about a lake, a mum, two boys and stepping in to help.

It's a warm summer's day in the early 1980s. The big brother and the little brother play together by a lake despite the whole two years and eight months that separate them. A fact of time that both brothers can instantly recall. Their mum has one eye on a situation unfolding in the lake and one on her boys – she is focused.

'ALISTER, look after Neil, NOW, I need to help', I hear my mum shout. The fear and resolve in her voice resonate in my mind as I watch her swim into the lake. Alister holds my forearm as big brothers do. We watch.

The water is cold, and the child who is drowning is just a few lengths in front of her.

Soon the child is now wrapped safely under one of her arms as she turns to check her boys are where she left them. They both look at her, waiting for their mum to swim back to them.

I didn't realise then that my mum taught me an important lesson in leadership – the importance of *side-step help*. A lesson about paying attention and being ready to step in.

I have tried to write the book that I looked for when I became a headteacher, something with simple lessons about what it is really like to be a new school leader. Thoughts of *'what do I do now?'* dominated my thinking when I got the job. And

I remember answering this question regularly, with a very simple phrase: *'be positive, be confident and be clear'*.

This book has taken this further by exploring four areas of learning to lead.

1. Doubt is something that we face as new and experienced leaders.
2. Challenges are a routine part of leadership and something to embrace in the privilege of leading.
3. Then, you need to learn the basics of leading every day and the importance of culture.
4. Behind that is the mindset you adopt as a leader.

None of this is complex, just simple lessons based on lived experience, through which I tried to answer the question *'what do I do now?'*

When we interview colleagues for leadership positions, I ask them to explain three things that make them effective leaders. You can answer this question in so many ways. Indeed, this book explores 49 different reflections on leadership.

I have moved beyond saying *'be positive, confident, and clear'*. My answer now to *'what now?'* has three parts. First, *ask for help*. Leadership is a heavy weight, and you can simply do it better with the help of others.

Second, *be curious*. Ask questions, enquire and be fanatical about finding out. By seeking to understand the causes of things and showing an interest, you can then effect positive change.

Finally, the lesson from the lake – the fiftieth reflection. Leaders need to be nimble and ready to *side-step help*. You must be ready to sort something here, quickly, to help something over there that is just as important – just like my mum did going into the lake and like great leaders do all the time.

I hope that *New School Leader: What Now?* has helped you to find positive answers. Schools need leaders like you who embrace the challenges of stepping up and who never forget the privilege of leading.

AFTERWORD

I joined a webinar with a leading expert in special educational needs, a parent and a student from Oxford University to talk about the impact of the pandemic on mental health. The host was seeking views from each participant, and we explored a range of issues, not least the impact of such high-stakes examinations at 16 and 18 years old in the UK. In the summer of 2022, it was the first time in three years that exams were going ahead. A typical 16-year-old takes approximately 25 exams and an 18-year-old taking A levels will take the best part of ten exams.

The student had an interesting backstory, having experienced exams being cancelled and receiving teacher-assessed grades in 2021. She told a story about how hard she'd worked at school and how disappointment followed when she couldn't sit her exams. She described how the period when schools were collecting evidence to grade pupils felt like one long examination period, much longer than the typical summer period of exams.

After the first lockdown, schools returned in September and spent the entire year collecting evidence in case exams were cancelled again. When the government cancelled the exams for the second time in January 2021, this just resulted in more internal tests for pupils. This successful young person made it though, achieving the highest teacher-assessed grades, and achieving her place at Oxford University.

The student recalled how she arrived at the university, proud of what she had achieved until she heard a group of older students deriding the new students because *'they hadn't sat real exams'*. I couldn't believe what she had just said. Listening to her story was a sobering reminder that, whether sitting exams or not, we have an accountability and examination system that puts incredible pressure on young people. She described how the comment tormented her and she looked forward to proving herself in real exams. She needed to shake the doubt that she was good enough.

Things have looked different in schools since the pandemic. Yes, there are positives. We saw children being pleased to be back in school with things getting back to normal. We saw engagement in extra-curricular activities increase. Year 11 and Year 13 pupils showed incredible resilience in the face of the first set of exams in three years. They really tackled them head-on and seized every opportunity for additional support. We arranged additional revision sessions at Easter and, within hours of publishing the sessions, families had booked their places. We arranged pre-examination technique sessions, where teachers briefed the pupils with final tips and techniques before pupils went into the exam hall. These were voluntary, but pupils turned up.

Many of the positive practices we developed during the pandemic have remained in school. Parents praised online parent meetings for their efficiency, no long queues, no travelling to school and the easier juggling of family life. Teachers felt online parent meetings helped their load as it was easier to keep to time and, for some who lived nearby, they could deliver them at home. We kept parents' evenings online. The catch-up funds helped, and we paid our teachers, who knew our pupils best, to deliver additional tuition. We kept the systems that we put in place, as we now know how to target precisely that additional help.

Despite these positives, some children have fallen more behind than others. Furthermore, we are yet to see the full impact of lockdowns on children in the early years of their primary education coming through into secondary schools. During the exams we saw more children needing additional access arrangements such as separate rooms due to anxiety. More children have presented with issues around their mental health, and we have funded additional hours of counselling to help. And, despite our best efforts, disadvantage continues to blight the education of so many. Disadvantage correlates so closely with lower levels of attendance, higher levels of suspension, lower reading age and lower levels of attainment.

We saw virtually no movement of staff during the pandemic, but we now see much more. People now have the confidence to move jobs and secure promotions. Some staff have reviewed their work-life balance post-Covid and left teaching. Normally, we would pull a field easily together when recruiting teachers, but this is getting more and more difficult. The teacher recruitment crisis is genuine in schools. We need to do more to recruit, retain and look after our teachers if we are to build a better society for our children and all our futures.

There is unquestionably a long shadow of the pandemic on pupils and staff who work in schools. The challenge of shadows is that they are very hard to research, and you catch only fleeting glimpses when the light is right. It is crucial that we understand the longer-term effects in school so leaders can be ready to adapt and collaborate with each other to support children.

There are a few very important things that educators should address that could profoundly improve the life chances of children. I recognise that each one is complex but nonetheless worthy of our collective action. I encourage new and established leaders to make them their focus.

First, we need a genuine review of the volume and nature of formal examinations in the UK. Is the current system fit for purpose and worthy of the children that take them?

Second, we need to tackle the variation that exists within and between schools. We need to discover ways to address this without creating winners and losers. The high-stakes nature of Ofsted and the reductionistic judgement of a school to one or two words – outstanding, good, requires improvement or inadequate – needs to develop to positively help address the variation.

Finally, educators talk about closing the gap between disadvantaged and non-disadvantaged children. We need a higher aspiration than this if we are to do justice to all children – our aspiration should be zero gaps. Success should not be a little narrowing of the gap, but zero gaps. We must expect more of the government and we must look to each other as leaders of schools, working in collaboration and with the purpose of driving change.

As educators, we influence the future – every day our teachers have an influence that reaches far into the future. Yet our thinking in schools remains entirely short-term. We think of the school year – 39 weeks of teaching, 195 days, some of these training days. We work by preparing students for the end-of-year exams. Our school improvement plans focus on one to three years, and if we are bold and talk about a long-term vision, we might look ten years into the future. The whole accountability system, recruitment crisis, workload and the plethora of other issues lock us entirely into very short-term thinking. We focus only on the present. What impact could we have, though, if we thought much more deeply about the long-term future, and the lives of children not yet born? What decisions could we make now as leaders in schools that could benefit children in a hundred years, or more?

William MacAskill (2022) in *What We Owe the Future*, puts forwards the idea that a clear moral priority of our time is to influence the long-term future. Future lives count for no less than those of the present generation, and their future could be good or bad. But we can make a positive difference in the future they experience. His perspective of *long termism*, applied to education, represents an exciting way of thinking for new leaders who can have an impact far beyond the generation we currently teach.

There are two areas to consider. First, what do we teach? How do we build a curriculum that delivers a rigorous understanding of values for the present and future such as equality, diversity, inclusion, sustainability and innovation? If we teach our children this well, they will teach theirs and future values become locked-in that positively benefit generation after generation.

Second, how do we fund schools? Many issues seem to come down to poor funding. There never seems to be enough money in the system to fund what needs to be done to tackle the issues that seem only to store up longer-term issues for society. Maybe we should be more sympathetic about how we have organised ourselves as a society to fund schools, because we haven't actually been doing this for very long.

My school started in 1903 and state organised schooling is relatively new in the history of society. Indeed, it is not until the 1880s that education became compulsory in England for children aged 5–10 and then up to 18 by 2015. We have only had 140 years to get this right and, it seems, we fund the present badly, let alone think about the future generously. But what if the first-ever headteacher of my school in 1903 were to have set up a fund each year that a headteacher couldn't use until 100 years later? What if I did this now? If I were to place the funds for one school child out of the 2100 children in the school, every year, for 100 years, how much funding would there be for the headteacher in 2123?

The headline funding figure for 2023–24 is £7460 per pupil. If I were to set up a fund, investing this amount once a year for

100 years, with a compound interest rate of 3 per cent, what would it be worth?

Recognising this is an estimate, the fund would have £5,043,084.62 available. Imagine the impact if we could organise ourselves as a society to invest even more than one pupil a year in a secondary school for the future lives of children that don't yet exist. What would education look like and what could our future society be if there was no such thing as a *'funding crisis in schools'*? The Greek proverb captures this so clearly: *'a society grows great when people plant trees under whose shade they will never sit'*. We need to think more creatively, not just about the present, but about the future.

This book is my story about how I tried to find answers to the question *'what now?'* as a new leader. My experience was made challenging because of the pandemic, an Ofsted inspection and the everyday running of our school. One thing that would help new leaders would be creative collective action to tackle the funding and recruitment crises in teaching. We must put the very best teachers in front of children, and we must think more boldly about the long-term future. This would make leading schools so much easier for leaders now and in the future. New leaders need to stay positive, be confident, drive development and stay humble. New leaders must look outwards and go beyond their own schools to help others if we are to build an education system that works for all.

New leaders should never forget what a privilege it is to lead, serve and care for their staff and students. New leaders should remind themselves every day of the power of education to transform lives. New leaders and schools must work together to build the future children deserve and develop the knowledge, skills and values our society so vitally needs.

REFERENCES

Bernstein, B (1964) Elaborated and Restricted Codes: Their Social Origins and Some Consequences. *American Anthropologist*, 66(6), Part 2: 55–69. doi: 10.1525/aa.1964.66.suppl_3.02a00030

Chang, J (1992) *Wild Swans: Three Daughters of China*. London: Harper Collins.

Cooley, C H (1902) *Human Nature and the Social Order.* New York: Charles Scribner's Sons.

Garfinkel, H (1967) *Studies in Ethnomethodology*. Cambridge: Polity Press.

Giddens, A (ed) (1972) *Emile Durkheim: Selected Writings*. Cambridge: Cambridge University Press.

Goffman, E (1959) *The Presentation of Self in Everyday Life*. London: Penguin.

MacAskill, W (2022) *What We Owe the Future: A Million-Year View*. Oxford: Oneworld Publications.

Mandela, N (1995) *Long Walk to Freedom*. London: Abacus.

Mead, G H (1934) *Mind, Self, and Society: From the Standpoint of a Social Behaviorist*. Chicago: University of Chicago Press.

Munby, S (2019) *Imperfect Leadership: A Book for Leaders Who Know They Don't Know It All*. Carmarthen: Crown House Publishing.

Rosenthal, R and Jacobson, L (1968) *Pygmalion in the Classroom: Teacher Expectation and Pupils' Intellectual Development*. New York: Holt, Rinehart and Winston.

Schools Week (2021) Downgraded 'Outstanding' Schools May Have Actually Improved, Says Ofsted Director'. [online] Available at: https://schoolsweek.co.uk/downgraded-outstanding-schools-may-have-actually-improved-says-ofsted-director/ (accessed 29 April 2023).

TES (2022) Ofsted: Half of 'Outstanding' Schools Downgraded. [online] Available at: www.tes.com/magazine/news/general/ofsted-half-outstanding-schools-downgraded (accessed 29 April 2023).

ADDITIONAL RESOURCES

Useful books for new leaders

Bartram, D (2018) *Great Expectations: Leading an Effective SEND Strategy in School*. London: Hachette.

Brady, K (2012a) *Karren Brady's 10 Rules for Success*. London: Harper Collins.

Brady, K (2012b) *Strong Woman: Ambition, Grit and a Great Pair of Heels*. London: Collins.

Buck, A (2018) *Leadership Matters 3.0: How Leaders at All Levels Can Create Great Schools*. Woodbridge: John Catt Educational.

Buck, A, Gibbons, R, Caviglioli, O and Roche, F (2019) *Honk!: When Teams Come Together, Organisations Fly*. Woodbridge: John Catt Educational.

Buck, A (2020) *The BASIC Coaching Method: All You Need to Know to Coach with Confidence.* Oxfordshire: Cadogan Press.

Cabane, O F (2012) *The Charisma Myth: Master the Art of Personal Magnetism*. London: Penguin.

Carter, D and McInerney, L (2020) *Leading Academy Trusts: Why Some Fail, But Most Don't*. Woodbridge: John Catt Educational.

Charvet, S R (2019) *Words that Change Minds: The 14 Patterns for Mastering the Language of Influence*. USA: Institute for Influence.

Collins, J (2011) *Good to Great: Why Some Companies Make the Leap ... And Others Don't*. London: Harper Collins.

Covey, S R (2013) *The 7 Habits of Highly Effective People: Powerful Lessons in Personal Change*. New York: Simon and Schuster.

Dweck, C S (2017) *Changing the Way You Think to Fulfil Your Potential*. London: Robinson.

Eddy, B (2011) *Biff: Quick Responses to High Conflict People, Their Hostile Emails, Personal Attacks and Social Media Meltdowns*. Arizona: HCI Press.

Ferriss, T (2016) *Tools of Titans: The Tactics, Routines, and Habits of Billionaires, Icons, and World-Class Performers*. London: Vermilion.

Gallo, C (2014) *Talk Like TED: The 9 Public Speaking Secrets of the World's Top Minds*. London: Pan Macmillan.

Gladwell, M (2008) *Outliers: The Story of Success*. London: Penguin.

Goyder, C (2014) *Gravitas: Communicate with Confidence, Influence and Authority*. London: Random House.

Granville-Chapman, K and Bidston, E (2020) *Leader: Know, Love and Inspire Your People*. Carmarthen: Crown House Publishing.

Hall, K and Hall, A (2017) *Kill Bad Meetings: Cut 50% of Your Meetings to Transform Your Culture, Improve Collaboration, and Accelerate Decisions*. London: Hachette.

Huffington, A (2014) *Thrive: The Third Metric to Redefining Success and Creating a Happier Life*. London: Random House.

Humphrey, J and Hughes, D (2021) *High Performance: Lessons from the Best on Becoming Your Best*. London: Random House.

Karia, A (2015) *TED Talks Storytelling: 23 Storytelling Techniques from the Best TED Talks*. California: Createspace Independent Publishing Platform.

Lencioni, P M (2010) *The Five Dysfunctions of a Team: A Leadership Fable, 20th Anniversary Edition*. Chichester: John Wiley & Sons.

Levitt, S D, Stern, F and Dubner, S J (2005) *Freakonomics: A Rogue Economist Explores the Hidden Side of Everything*. Berlin: Walter de Gruyter.

Murphy, P W (2012) *Always Know what to Say: Easy Ways to Approach and Talk to Anyone*. Amazon Digital Services.

Nanson, P (2019) *Stand Up Straight: 10 Life Lessons from the Royal Military Academy Sandhurst*. London: Random House.

Pang, A S-K (2016) *Rest: Why You Get More Done When You Work Less*. London: Penguin.

Porritt, V and Featherstone, K (2019) *10% Braver: Inspiring Women to Lead Education*. London: SAGE.

Rogelberg, S G (2019) *The Surprising Science of Meetings: How You Can Lead Your Team to Peak Performance*. New York: Oxford University Press.

Sandberg, S (2013) *Lean In: Women, Work, and the Will to Lead*. London: Random House.

Sandberg, S and Grant, A (2017) *Option B: Facing Adversity, Building Resilience, and Finding Joy*. London: Random House.

Schmidt, E, Rosenberg, J and Eagle, A (2019) *Trillion Dollar Coach: The Leadership Handbook of Silicon Valley's Bill Campbell*. London: Hachette.

Sinek, S (2011) *Start with Why: How Great Leaders Inspire Everyone to Take Action*. London: Penguin.

Sinek, S (2014) *Leaders Eat Last: Why Some Teams Pull Together and Others Don't*. London: Penguin.

Stanier, M B (2016) *The Coaching Habit: Say Less, Ask More & Change the Way You Lead Forever*. Vancouver: Page 2.

Stanier, M B (2020) *The Advice Trap: Be Humble, Stay Curious & Change the Way You Lead Forever*. Vancouver: Page 2.

Steward, J (2018) *Sustaining Resilience in Leadership: Stories from Education*. London: Hachette.

Syed, M (2011) *Bounce: The Myth of Talent and the Power of Practice*. London: Fourth Estate.

Syed, M (2016) *Black Box Thinking: Marginal Gains and the Secrets of High Performance.* London: John Murray.

Thaler, R H and Sunstein, C R (2012) *Nudge: The Final Edition.* London: Penguin.

Tomsett, J and Uttley, J (2020) *Putting Staff First: A Blueprint for Revitalising Our Schools.* Woodbridge: John Catt Educational.

Tracy, B (2013) *Eat that Frog!: 21 Great Ways to Stop Procrastinating and Get More Done in Less Time.* London: Hodder & Stoughton.

Tuhovsky, I (2015) *Communication Skills Training: A Practical Guide to Improving Your Social Intelligence, Presentation, Persuasion and Public Speaking.* CreateSpace Independent Publishing Platform.

Twitter

Who to follow to make your Twitter account all about education:

@ASCL_UK
@profbeckyallen
@EducEndowFounn
@Carter6D
@Dylanwiliam
@educationgovuk
@GuardianEdu
@Headteacherchat
@Headrest_UK
@HeadsRoundtable
@JohnDunford
@JohnTomsett
@JonnyUttley
@juliecmcculloch
@Louis Everett
@MaryMyatt
@miss_mcinerney
@Ofstednews

@Ofqual
@PaulGarvey4
@ProfCoe
@Rachel_deSouza
@RealGeoffBarton
@ResearchED1
@RossMcGill
@SecEd-Education
@SchoolsWeek
@Seizingsuccess
@Steve_munby
@Strickomaster
@TeachFirst
@Teacherhead
@TeacherTapp
@TeacherToolkit
@UKEdChat
@womened

Podcasts on leadership

The introvert leader podcast
Vivienne Porritt 10% braver podcast
Diary of a CEO
High-Performance Podcast

Other organisations

Ambition Institute – professional development programmes support teachers and school leaders www.ambition.org.uk

Association of School and College Leaders www.ascl.org.uk

Charted College – useful Impact journal supports the teaching community by connecting research findings to classroom practice www.chartered.college

Education Endowment Foundation – supports schools to improve teaching and learning through better use of evidence www.educationendowmentfoundation.org.uk

Headrest – offer a free 24/7 well-being telephone support service for headteachers www.headrestuk.co.uk

Leadership Matters – helps leadership development via diagnostic tools www.leadershipmatters.org.uk

Useful books and resources about teaching and learning

Allison, S, Tharby, A and Lemov, D (2015) *Making Every Lesson Count: Six Principles to Support Great Teaching and Learning*. Carmarthen: Crown House Publishing.

Didau, D (2019) *Making Kids Cleverer: A Manifesto for Closing the Advantage Gap*. Carmarthen: Crown House Publishing.

Kirschner, P A and Hendrick, C (2020) *How Learning Happens: Seminal Works in Educational Psychology and what They Mean in Practice*. London: Routledge.

Lemov, D (2021) *Teach Like a Champion 3.0: 63 Techniques that Put Students on the Path to College*. Chichester: John Wiley & Sons.

Nuthall, G (2007) *The Hidden Lives of Learners*. Wellington: Nzcer Press.

Quigley, A (2018) *Closing the Vocabulary Gap*. London: Routledge.

Quigley, A (2020) *Closing the Reading Gap*. London: Routledge.

Sherrington, T (2017) *The Learning Rainforest: Great Teaching in Real Classrooms*. Woodbridge: John Catt Educational.

Weinstein, Y, Sumeracki, M and Caviglioli, O (2018) *Understanding How We Learn: A Visual Guide*. London: Routledge.

Willingham, D T (2009) *Why Don't Students Like School?: A Cognitive Scientist Answers Questions About How the Mind Works and What It Means for the Classroom*. Chichester: John Wiley & Sons.

Podcasts about teaching and learning

Becoming Educated – Darren Leslie
Education Research Reading Room – Ollie Lovell
Mind The Gap – Tom Sherrington and Emma Turner
Mr Barton Maths Podcast – Craig Barton
SENDcast – The Podcast for Special Educational Needs and Disability (SEND)
Teacher toolkit podcast

Blogs/Articles

A Chemical Orthodoxy – Adam Boxer www.achemicalorthodoxy.wordpress.com/
Mary Myatt www.marymyatt.com/blog
American Educator, 2012. Principles of Instruction: Research-Based Strategies That All Teachers Should Know. [online] Available at: www.aft.org/sites/default/files/Rosenshine.pdf (accessed 29 April 2023).
American Educator, 2013. Strengthening the Student Toolbox: Study Strategies to Boost Learning. [online] Available at: https://files.eric.ed.gov/fulltext/EJ1021069.pdf (accessed 29 April 2023).

INDEX

allies, importance of, 7–9
ambitions, 151–3
anomie, 171
appreciation, 95–7, 143
arrogance-veil trap, 33, 34
assertion, 48–50

benches, 158–60
bias, 19
brain science, 149
brave individuals, 90
breathing, 57

calm mind, 56–9
carrying on, 125–7
colleagues, 7–9, 73
collective conscience, 86–7
communication, 56–9
communication issue, 48
complaints, resolving, 54–5
concentrated listening, 54
courage, 59–61
covering off, 45–7
Covid-19 pandemic, impact of, 192–4

creativity, 102
curiosity, 85–7, 190

decision-making, 18–21, 24, 49
difficult conversations, 44
disadvantaged and non-disadvantaged children, closing the gap between, 195
discussing and sharing with others, 102
Durkheim, E, 86, 171

echo technique, 54–5
effective decisions, 19
effective time management, 117
elaborate speech code, 12
emotions, 57
empathy, 183
empowerment, 110–12
ethnomethodology, 114
evidence-based reports, 49, 50

failure, handling, 128–31
fallacy of stepping forward, 108

feedback
- from closest colleagues, 7–9
- concept and principles, 104–6

forgetting, 28–30
fragile strengths, 180, 183
funding, 196–7
future, planning for, 195–6

gestures, 92
goals, 141–2
gratitude, 95–7, 146
Green Cross Code, 60

hard decisions, 19
help, asking for, 33–5, 190
Higgins, Rob, 186–7
humility, 33
humour, use of, 7

identification skill, 33
imposter syndrome, 11
improver-learner, 90
information
- and effective judgement, 19
- valid sources of, 49

inspection, 62–74

joined-up individuals, 90
judgements, 19

Kopfkino, 25–7, 165

Lake Wobegon Effect, 116, 120
language, importance of, 46
leadership position, taking up, 5–6
life chances of children, improving, 194–5
little things, significance of, 143–4, 174
long termism, 196
looking glass self, 54, 55

Meadus, Emma, 135–6
meetings, 116
- avoiding bias, 118
- avoiding distractions, 117
- complexity of, 116
- evaluation of, 119–20
- fostering positive conflict and forging effective participation, 118
- handling Any Other Business, 120
- making others the priority, 116–17
- seeking agreement but recognising when to direct, 119
- time management, 117

memorial benches, 159

mental health support, 60
mentors, 34
Mind, Self and Society (Mead), 92
mistakes, reflecting on, 114
misunderstanding, 53–5
moments of perspective, 132–3
motivated forgetting, 28, 29
Multi-Academy Trusts (MATs), 181–2

natural potential, 181
negative thoughts, 11
negativity, 51, 148–50
networks, 34, 178
next steps, 107–9
'no,' saying, 168–9

Odin Development Compass, 180
opener questions, 98–9
optimism, 148–50
organisational feedback, 104
organised, being, 113–15
others' views, seeking, 49

Parkinson's Law, 117
Partington, Matthew, 79–80
pause and launch approach, 152–3

personal feedback, 104
perspective
    keeping, 51–2
    moments of, 132–3
pipelines, 176–9
plain speaking, 12–14
planning, 89
poor decisions, 19
positive narratives, 148–50
positive thinking, 51–2
potential outcomes, assessing, 25
praise, 10–11, 143
preoccupation, 32
preparation, 113–15
pressure, working under, 62–74
pride, 10, 143
problem, sharing the, 34
process, 88–91

Quarmby, Gemma, 37–8
questioner-challengers, 90
questions, 98–100
quiet ambitions, 151–3
quiet-perceptive individuals, 89

reading, 122–4
recognition, 143
reification of trusts, 182
relationships, 65

remembering, 28–30
responsibility, 5–6, 22, 105, 114, 162
rest, 75–7
restarting, 128–31
restricted speech code, 12, 13
revealer questions, 99
risk-taking, measured, 164–6

safe-option, 165
school trips, 101–3
seeker questions, 99
self, presentation of, 8
self-doubt, 11
self-employed mindset, 161–3
    pitfall of, 167–9
    and risk-taking, 166
self-preservation, 29
shame, 10, 11
side-step help, 189, 190
sideways working, 180–4
smiling, 92–4
social change, coping with, 45–7
social interaction, 92
solidarity, 72
solution-faced approach, 46
speaking
    from the heart, 15–17
    plain, 12–14

speech codes, 12
standards setting, 173–5
steppingstones, helping to cross, 110–12
strong leadership, misconception of, 154–7

task-ticker-type leaders, 162
thanking, 95–7
threads, 170–2
three-fold thanks, 96
trust, 65, 90, 145–7

underperformance, facing head-on, 43–4
understanding skill, 53–5
unintended consequences, 46, 62
U-turns, 22–4

visibility, 31–2
visits, 101–3
vulnerability, 33

walkabout visits, 102
weight of responsibility, 5–6

'yes,' saying, 168

zero-gaps thread, 171, 195

For Product Safety Concerns and Information please contact our EU
representative GPSR@taylorandfrancis.com
Taylor & Francis Verlag GmbH, Kaufingerstraße 24, 80331 München, Germany

www.ingramcontent.com/pod-product-compliance
Lightning Source LLC
Chambersburg PA
CBHW060605230426
43670CB00011B/1972